LOVE AND LOVE'S ENERGY

RAVENSOUND
PUBLISHING

LOVE
–AND–
LOVE'S ENERGY

How Attachment Science Proves That Love Nurtures Our Biological Nature, Impacts Our Positive View of Ourselves, of Others, and of God, and Teaches Us All How to Love.

Tara Boothby

MA Psychology. BA Theology.
Registered Psychologist

Copyright © Tara Boothby 2024.

All rights reserved. No part of this publication may be reproduced, distributed, or transmitted in any form or by any means, without prior written permission of the respective author.

Author email: tara.boothby@sojo.ca

Ravensound Publishing
Brisbane, QLD, Australia

Cover art by Jared Robinson
Title: Heart Core
www.JaredRobinson.ca
@jaredRobinsonArt
Copyright © 2024

Typesetting & design: David Tensen davidtensen.com

Also available in eBook

Love & Love's Energy/ Tara Boothby. -- 1st ed

ISBN 978-1-7382439-0-7

Dedication

To the dappled,
The damaged,
The broken.

To the wounded and
To the forgotten.

To the lonely.

To no one and
To every one.

But most of all
To you;
Just the way you are.

To you, and
For you,
I write this book, because
You too are
Loved, loveable and loving.

And I am very glad you are here.

Love you,
Tara

Table of Contents

ENDORSEMENTS VIII

AN INTRODUCTION TO LOVE

WHAT IS LOVE? 3
RESOUNDING CHURCH BELLS 9
WHAT DOES LOVE DO FOR US? 13
HOW DOES LOVE WORK? 19
A WORD ABOUT G-O-D 23

LOVED

BEING HUMAN 29
YOUR SIDE OF THE STREET 31
DEFAULT STRATEGIES 39
I BELONG ALONE 49
OUR FEAR 57
PURE-OF-HEART 59
EXISTENTIAL CRISIS, SHIFTS, & EPIPHANY 63
YOU GET TO CHOOSE WHO YOU ARE IN
ALL OF YOUR RELATIONSHIPS 67
EMOTIONAL SAFETY 75

LOVEABLE

A LIFELONG LOVE STORY 83
NATURE, NURTURE, AND THE HEART OF LOVE 85
NURTURING ATTACHMENTS 93
PARENT GUILT 101
PARENTAL VALUE 111
FORGOTTEN MIRACLES 117
NEVER TOO LATE 121

LOVING

LOVE FOR YOU & ME	129
BEING BORN	131
SELF-LOVE	139
SELF-COMPASSION & EMPATHY	143
THE MYSTERY OF SELF-LOVE	147
SHAME, GUILT, HUMILIATION	155
A NOTE ON VULNERABILITY	161
THE GOOD AND THE BAD DOG	165
THE MAGIC MAGNET	169
A NOTE ON TRAUMA	175
A LITTLE ROOM IN OUR BRAIN	177
BEYOND FORGIVENESS	185
REPAIR	191
A CONTEMPLATION FOR RECONCILIATION	197

LOVE'S ENERGY

FALLING INTO LOVE	203
A NEW VIEW OF LOVE	207
YOU ARE LOVED, LOVEABLE, & LOVING	211
BEING INCLUDED IN LOVE'S HEART	217
GOD'S LOVE IS LOVING	221
CAN GOD BE LOVING AND CORRECTING?	227
INDISCRIMINATE LOVE	231
IS GOD REALLY LOVING?	237

TYING IT IN A BOW

TREADING WATER	245
A LETTER FROM WM. PAUL YOUNG	253
ACKNOWLEDGEMENTS	255
SUGGESTED READING AND BIBLIOGRAPHY	259

Endorsements

"This is a little book with big ideas. It is also a symphony of love. Tara challenges us to reimagine Love as Love's Energy, hardwired in us for each other and for our personal ability to embrace broken, messy parts of ourselves. Love is beyond words; it can only be experiencing as an epiphany of something generative and transformative with all our being, our whole selves. It takes a spiritual lens and a dialectical way of thinking to understand love as the most powerful force for healing, growing, flourishing and co-creating a better world, because the space between God and humans, between individuals and between the light and shadow within the self is both irreducible and inseparable; both sacred and terrifying. I highly recommend this book to everyone who wants to experience love in all its splendor in a safe space provided by Tara Miller Boothby."

Dr. Paul T. P. Wong

Professor Emeritus, Trent University and Trinity Western University.
Originator of the Integrative Meaning Therapy; Founding President of the International Network on Personal Meaning, and Author.

"Tara begs the question 'can we learn to be completely loved by God?' I say what a great subject! Have I learned to be completely loved by God?' and, 'To whatever degree I have, how did I get here?'

To trust God is to experience being loved by God. To turn away to our own devices and control is to orient ourselves toward the shadowlands where our sense of Love's Energy is diminished, and we become lost and confused. Of course, God's love is always a constant, but in our turning and orientation away our awareness of that Love fades. Love and Love's Energy is a book where we can consider human love and God's always constant love-energy."

William Paul Young
Best Selling Author of "The Shack".

"A compelling and soulful invitation to find love, to see we belong, and to know we are beloved. Love and Love's Energy is a powerful discovery of the everyday presence of love in life. Tara Boothby invites us to a whole-hearted journey toward the power and the promise of love. Not as a possession or achievement, but an everyday gift that transcends troubles, animates hope, and leads one back to the heart of divine love."

James Furrow PhD.
ICEFFT Trainer and Supervisor, Author, and Coauthor of "Emotionally Focused Family Therapy: Restoring Connections and Promoting Resilience,"
Researcher, and Former Freed Professor of Marital and Family Therapy at Fuller Theological Seminary, Pasadena, CA.

"Tara Boothby in her book, Love and Love's Energy gently nudges us to take a deep dive into the human and spiritual experience of love. She generously shares her personal stories and learnings with the reader and helps us understand and accept what it is like to be loved, lovable and loving. Her writing transmits what she describes as love-energy and challenges us to take the risk to fearlessly question and examine the world of love."

Gail Palmer
MSW, RMFT, ICEEFT Trainer, Supervisor, Therapist, Coauthor of Emotionally Focused Family Therapy: Restoring Connections and Promoting Resilience."

"In this hostile era where Love is increasingly seen through cynical eyes as idealistic and ineffectual, we need Tara Boothby's timely reminder that, in truth, there is no energy more powerful. The energy of Love undergirds and permeates the cosmos and can penetrate the innermost being of any human being to heal and transform. Tara is not naive about human wreckage and doesn't peddle platitudes. She knows the healing power of love from her direct experience as a clinical practitioner. An accessible and hopeful book."

Dr. Bradley Jersak
President, St. Stephen's University (NB, Canada); Author of "IN: Incarnation & Inclusion, Abba & Lamb".

"I appreciate Tara Boothby's beautiful and thorough attempt to convince us that we are all loved, lovable, and loving (starting with ourselves) .... something everyone in this world very much needs to believe."

David Hayward, aka NakedPastor,
Author of "Flip It Like This!"

"From the initial chapter to the closing sentiment, reading this text was truly delightful. Yet, this doesn't come as a surprise, given Tara's profound understanding of love and attachment. Tara's warmth, passion, wisdom, and creativity resonate on every page. This is a must-read for anyone embarking on a quest to delve deeper into the realms of love, attachment, and the essence of being human."

Robin Williams Blake
Registered Psychotherapist, ICEEFT Trainer and Supervisor
Associate Graduate Faculty - Wilfrid Laurier University

"I love Tara's book on a personally level, as a therapist, and as a person, on an emotional journey. It is a smooth read and it invokes emotions. Love and Love's Energy highlights the benefit and importance of love and attachment for healthy relationships."

Lena Santhirasegaram
MC, RP.,CCC., Prov. Psychologist,
Board Certified in Neurofeedback, Senior Fellow

"Much love for Love and Love's Energy. The heart and hard earned years of wisdom of a practicing Psychologist, Tara Boothby, shine through to illuminate one of lives most challenging and important mysteries, love. Tara has written a masterpiece balancing faith, practical and attainable knowledge of our most important relationships while balancing the contributions of legitimate science. This balance is rare, valuable and much needed; a huge contribution to a world in need."

Ryan Rana
PhD; LMFT-S, LPC-S AR; ICEEFT Trainer and Supervisor,
Codirector of The Joshua Center, Arkansa,
Podcasts: Success In Vulnerability, and The Leading Edge

"There is much compact and whispered wisdom in Tara Boothby's Love and Love's Energy—the dives go deep, many finely polished pearls held graciously and exquisitely shared in the surfacing. The journey taken in the book is personal and yet also perennial for the simple reason the more the true gold of love and love's energy is mined, the more it speaks to one and all in their human longings on our all too human journey---do read and meditatively digest this beauty of a book—eyes rinsed in the process and the dynamic of authentic love birthed---a fine midwife of a book."

Ron Dart
Professor Emeritus University of the Fraser Valley; Professor Saint Stephen's University; National Executive of The Thomas Merton Society of Canada

Endorsement For *Love and Love's Energy* by the Scaffolding Partners of this book:

"Tara's work both asks and answers the question of how Love's Energy pulses through all things. The rhythm she adopts writing in prose, poetry, and professional insight gives nuance to this important message. I am grateful this book is in the world as a kind of bright highlighter, drawing our attention to the ways Love hides in plain sight, every day."

David Tensen
Ravensound Publishing, Publisher for Love and Love's Energy;
Poet and Author of "The Wrestle."

"Boothby delivers us an invitation to consider our whole selves without discarding any part of us. All is welcome in the journey - flaws, fears, defaults. It is all included. Through the pages of her work the reader is encouraged to embrace their pure-of-heartness and to be reminded that we are all loved, loveable and loving. It's a book I'd want to hand to a friend if they were treading water in the difficulty of life's circumstances, to a friend asking for resources or materials to gain understanding and guidance. "

Felicia Murrell
Editor of Love and Love's Energy;
Author of "Truth Encounters" & "AND: The Restorative Power of Love in an Either/Or World."

"Tara captures the significance of love as she reveals that 'the space between people is sacred.' I appreciate the way she breathes life into our flat and physical 'Valentine's way' of understanding love, in order to see it as the transformative energy between Us."

Jared Robinson
Artist of "Heart Core" (Cover Art for Love and Love's Energy), Artist and Author of "God and Todd Create a Creature".

Love and Love's Energy

AN INTRODUCTION TO LOVE

"Fitting in is about assessing a situation and becoming who you need to be to be accepted. Belonging, on the other hand, doesn't require us to change who we are; it requires us to be who we are."
Brené Brown [1]

---

[1] Brené Brown (2021). Atlas of the Heart: Mapping Meaningful Connection and the Language of Human Experience. New York, Random House.

Love and Love's Energy

WHAT IS LOVE?

A few years ago, I wrote a short story called *Bear & Bunny*. This short story is about love and tells of two dear friends who are playing in the forest. When Bunny asks Bear to define love, Bear playfully explains to Bunny how the energy between the two animals is love.

> Bear says, *"I get a feeling in my tummy all warmy, tingly good."*

Bear's explanation may not hold great grammatical value, but for those of us who slow down to consider what love is, understanding love as energy makes sense. Bear is defining love in terms of the body sensations Bear feels at the precise moment when Bear notices *"I am included just the way I am."* Bear does not need words from Bunny. Bear senses into the moment of playing with Bunny and notices the energy that is within Bear's body. Bear trusts this energy is proof of Bunny's love. Bear trusts it is love for the sake of being loved.

> Have you ever had a feeling in your tummy all warmy, tingly good? This is the energy of love.

Speaking of love evokes a natural sense of curiosity. People long to have moments where we are heard, seen, and known—valued just as we are. We collect these moments and are soothed by them. The more moments where we experience being valued for no other reason than the reason we exist, the more we hope for these moments to occur again and again. We become aware of *"the feeling in our tummy,"* and we become better informed on our definition of love.

People are curious about love because it is an essential contribution to our survival. Our longing for moments energized by love is not superficial. As we are energized by love we have an assurance we are always included, just the way we are.

> Love is inviting and available. No matter the condition of our inner self. Love is loving.

Attachment is a term we will understand more through the pages of this book, it is the fuel of our nurture experience, the fuel of our *love-energy*. Nurture is our relational experiences from cradle to the grave, and it promotes or declines our born biological nature. Relationships have immense developmental and psychological value, and inescapable theological doing and undoing. After all, our relationships with other people imprint on all parts of who we are.

The space between people is sacred. In this space all this love stuff occurs. But this space is riddled with barriers and benefits, and then unique complexities. Each one of us is exploring the landscape of our relationship with ourselves, with others, and with God, at our own pace, and at our own level of awareness.

> Having a better understanding of love will aid us to be more conscious of all our relationships — the relationships we cherish, as well as the relationships we are desperate to escape.

Many of us do long to escape our relationships. This is okay, even healthy at times. Yet, it is still unnatural for people to be out of relationship, which contributes to us feeling unresolved and imbalanced in our longing for love, and imbalanced in our longing to escape love. When relationships fracture, even the worst relationships, it can be scary. We wonder *"What is wrong with me? What causes me to keep getting hurt by people? What causes me to keep hurting others? What keeps me hurting myself?"* Hurt is going to happen in relationships, then unremedied relational hurts festers and repeats.

Sometimes, we get hurt, and no one seems to notice. We may be left hurt and alone and begin wondering why we are hurt and alone. Most of us wonder if our being hurt and alone is due to our unique fallibility. Without the soothing love from another we are prone to more hurt and more isolation.

Being heard, seen, and known, in our times of pain soothes our fear that the worst about us is true.[1] In our time of pain when we are met with love by the people who matter most to us, we experience a glimmer of hope to try for love one more time. We become aware of how the energy of love feels.

Moments of fracture will happen in relationships. Resolving these moments fuels our *love-energy*. When these moments are left unresolved, we are left unresolved.

We want to be seen favorably, of course. *"The more favorably I am seen the more likely I will be loved, and the less risk of others realizing how flawed I truly am."*

However, the more we experience love, the better able we are to navigate the vulnerable experience of being a flawed and valuable person in relationships with other flawed and valuable people. Yes, we can be both flawed and valuable at the same time. We all have value. Our experiences, good and bad, have value. When we make peace with this flawed and valuable duality, we can develop a more intimate knowledge of

---

[1] Bowlby, John. (1988). A Secure Base: Parent-Child Attachment and Healthy Human Development. Basic Books.

what love is, to better see the *love-energy* that is all around us. Ultimately, we can live from a place where we know with our whole being that we are loved, loveable, and loving.

> The truth is: love does not belong to us; we belong to *Love*. Whether we fight it or not, we belong. We are valuable and valued. We do not need to gain perfection on the inside to participate in the *love-energy* all around us.

Love allows us to love ourselves, all of who we are, so we can learn to trust how all of the parts of who we are are loveable, even the worst parts—our flaws and fear, our personal version of "I belong alone," even our default strategies which we use to protect ourselves. We are loved just the way we are.

As love and Love's Energy becomes central to our existence, we change in so many ways. This love we are included in leads us to realize:

We are included in the same heart of love as everyone else.

We are loveable.

We are loved as whole people, not in part. As we love ourselves more,

We are loving of others.

We receive more love from others.

We repair some of our wounded relationships with others.

We repair our own wounded relationship with ourselves.

We learn what emotional safety means.

We see the mystery of love, Love we are participating in.

Love makes it safe to be curious and ask serious questions, like: What is love-energy and what is its source?

Throughout the book there will be contemplation questions like this one at the end of most chapters.

This book is a love discovery. Together we will discover proof of our loved, loveable, and loving identity. And together we will explore how belonging to emotionally safe *self-love* fosters hope for emotionally safe love with other people, which we call *love-energy*. This then, opens us up to wonder about the mystery of supernatural love; *Love's* grander *Energy*.

Love and Love's Energy

RESOUNDING CHURCH BELLS

There is nothing like walking down a foreign street in a foreign town on a Sunday morning when the different church bells chime and the sound carries through the air. Church bells resounding through the air is a welcome sound for me. I am always moved by the experience of hearing the bells ring and, at the same time, feeling the resounding vibrations inside my very being.

> The bells ring through the air and then the bells ring through me — a resounding.

Have you ever had this experience? Perhaps you have heard and felt bells ringing through the city streets or a singing bowl hit with a mallet and circled. Maybe it's the feeling of a favorite song, or some favorite sound you look forward to hearing throughout your day. Your ears perk up. Your nervous system responds. For me, the resounding feels a bit like butterflies in my stomach and a thick, brilliant sensation in my core, like breathing in intoxicating smoke. Not smoke from a fire or even from incense, but a pleasant foggy smoke that brings clarity to my being and my mind — it becomes an embodied moment.

> Resounding bells are a powerful experience, not necessarily religious, but spiritual — soulful. More than a noise to call our attention, the pleasant sound is accompanied by a resounding energy.

The sensation of church bells resounding inside of me reminds me of the power of attunement between people: when we *"get it right"* with someone else, when we *"show up"* in a relationship, when we hear someone, then at the same time really see them, or vice versa, when someone hears us and really sees us. These types of moments move through our bodies. These moments move through our shared relational space with another person, or at times with many people. In these times we all have an experience together— a resounding.

> When we have resounding moments, we share an energy experience with other people.

The resounding of the pleasant chime does not discriminate just as our capacity for resounding moments does not discriminate. I guess we might ignore such moments and so not consent to the resounding, we still do have a choice to participate. But when we do choose to listen, we are all included in the resounding of sound. The bells do not know what we are carrying around. The bells do not know if we have trauma or flaws, or if we have done terrible deeds, they ring, and continue ringing, right through us. Much like when we experience being heard and seen by another person and we experience being accepted *just the way we are* without the need to explain or hide our flaws. These moments are sacred — corrective. In these resounding moments we feel something we were meant to be acquainted with since the day we were born.

> It is natural to long for experiences where we will be joined by another in this resounding way.

I hope this book will ring through all of the parts of who you are. I hope this book will ring through you and your relationships with other people. I hope this book rings through you and your relationship with

God. I also hope you will keep in pace with yourself, let love ring through you, while maintaining your own emotional safety. There is no need to sprint. Most often, resounding moments happen as we stroll.

This is a book for those who want to know how deeply broken and messy we are in our own selves. A book for people willing to touch our own broken parts, and to admit we feel lonely. This is a book for people who want to know how to bring all of our broken bits along with us into all our relationships —when we can as we can. For now, let's slow down and allow all this talk of love to unfold. Go easy on yourself. Let whatever happens happen. Here, in the pages of this book, we get to discover what love is in a fresh way. Perhaps, in the pages of this book, we'll even begin experiencing love in a fresh way. Let whatever happens happen.

This book is written for you and me, *just the way we are*. I write this to you:

> *In the fullness of who you are as a whole person,*
>
> *No matter your flaws and defaults,*
>
> *No matter what fear has scripted about your identity.*
>
> *That you may have a renewed understanding of love.*
>
> *That you may become curious to accept your version of "I belong alone."*
>
> *That you may see you're valued,*
>
> *As you participate and belong in this great collective: Love.*

WHAT DOES LOVE DO FOR US?

"Love is not the limitation; love is the flying."
William Paul Young[1]

The goal of attachment experiences is to have corrective attachment epiphanies with the people we love.[2] A corrective epiphany is a moment. Oftentimes, a small moment. A moment that can go unnoticed if we do not slow down and help ourselves and our people to savor them. These moments are not mere therapy goals, these moments are life goals. Corrective epiphanies happen all around us. Kent Hoffman, one of the originators of the Circle of Security model for parenting, will say they are what is *hidden in plain sight*.[3]

> May we become better at noticing the moments in our lives that are doing something profound inside of us and the people we love.

These moments of epiphany are moments of resounding *love-energy*.

Corrective love epiphanies remind us we are not alone. These are *love-energy* moments. These moments are most obvious in close attachment relationships like parent and child, siblings, or spouses, but they occur all around us, in many different ways, in many

---

[1] Young, Wm. Paul (2007). *The Shack: Where Tragedy Confronts Eternity.* Windblown Media, Faithwords, Hodder & Stoughton.

[2] Johnson, Sue (2004). *The Practice of Emotionally Focused Couple Therapy: Creating Connections.* Routledge.

[3] Hoffman, Kent (2015). eightysevenminutes.com.

different relationships. In these moments, one person is met by another, and they experience being heard, seen, and known as a whole person without any inquiry as to whether they deserve to be met. Love meets us just the way we are.

> Love for the sake of love. Love in a way we all have longed for our entire life.

I am too mainstream and basic, and too conservative in my spiritual views, to call myself an energy worker, but I am just mystical enough to know attachment work is always all about energy. Scientifically, attachment work is rooted in how our central nervous systems (CNS) experience other people's CNS and the neurological process of how we make meaning of CNS co-regulation.[1] Biologically speaking, life is about self-regulation and co-regulation, the CNS and the neurology of our co-regulation, and our attachment systems.[2] The more corrective epiphanies we experience, the more regulated our CNS becomes, the better our CNS functions for the benefit of our entire being.

I am a person like every other human, my body already knows good transformative moments are all about an energy shift in my body. I also know good transformative moments are about an energy shift in your body. Your body has always known this, and now your mind does too. We are wired to not only experience these epiphanies but to notice their energy.

---

[1] Siegel, Daniel, Payne Bryson, Tina (2011). The Whole-Brain Child: 12 Revolutionary Strategies to Nurture Your Child's Developing Mind. Delacorte Press.

[2] Siegel, Daniel, Payne Bryson, Tina (2011). The Whole-Brain Child: 12 Revolutionary Strategies to Nurture Your Child's Developing Mind. Delacorte Press.

Can you think of any moments of corrective epiphanies— *resounding* — you have experienced?

Take as much time as you like to drift through key relationships in your life story. As you do, notice moments that have been corrective for you. Moments when you felt hope for your connection to other people. These corrective moments may include events like; *holding your child, catching your spouse's eye on your wedding day, having a big laugh with a dear friend, finding a note or treat on your office desk, a little hand in your hand, a heart-to-heart hug, a first kiss, someone remembering something you previously said, your pet greeting you at the door, dancing in the arms of someone who loves you, your parent's eyes on you in a time of achievement, being comforted when you cry, holding someone who is broken-hearted, a chuckle with a new friend.*

> Moments like these are good to take note of.
> These are positive experiences for us to dwell on.
> What other moments would you add to this list?

Love is a mighty force. The Song of Solomon compares love to the unyielding power of death.[1] Love has such a potent effect; it is even compared to the power of death! We fear dying, as we should. At times, we also fear the power of love. Love is powerful when it is done wrong, and love is powerful when it is done right.

---

[1] Peterson, Eugene H. (1993). The Message: The Bible in Contemporary Language. NavPress.

Attachment folks will say we see attachment in terms of life and death.[1] The absence of attachment is as all-consuming as death. Without being dramatic, there is a lot of science to prove this statement: without attachment, parts of our biology die off, our brain function will decrease, we may even completely lose some neurological function, our central nervous systems (CNS) will miss out on being regulated and soothed.[2] There are grave consequences to missing out on love.

Research confirms that loving relationships are vital to our existence and our development.[3] The absence of love means the absence of all the biological benefits of love. There is scientific proof that supports the value of *love-energy*.

---

[1] Johnson, Sue (2008). Hold Me Tight: Seven Conversations for a Lifetime of Love. Little, Brown Spark.

[2] Ainsworth (Salter), Mary, Blehar, Mary C., Waters, Everett, Wall, Sally (1979). *Patterns of Attachment: A Psychological Study of the Strange Situation*. Routledge.

[3] Siegel, Daniel, Payne Bryson, Tina (2011). The Whole-Brain Child: 12 Revolutionary Strategies to Nurture Your Child's Developing Mind. Delacorte Press.

Contemplative Questions:

Going forward when groups of questions like these show up, they are for you to do with as you please: read and write your answers, contemplate and answer to yourself, reflect with an emotionally safe person, or you may choose to ignore these questions if you do not find them useful. The choice is yours; this is your love journey.

What does love do for you?

Can you recall some examples of love epiphanies you have experienced?

What is your definition of *love-energy* at this point?

Love is powerful. It is something to be in awe of, or at least, to wonder about. Love is also corrective energy. But how does love work?

Love and Love's Energy

HOW DOES LOVE WORK?

"Being the "best you can be" is really only possible when you are deeply connected to another. Splendid isolation is for planets, not people."
Dr. Sue Johnson[1]

We all have experience of making mistakes. It is frightening to get things wrong. It is normal to wonder if others will turn away from us completely. We get things wrong, and on some level, we worry that people will stop loving us. When someone makes a mistake with us and we hear and see them through their perfectly-imperfect glorious identity, this is a moment of *love-energy*. When we are held in a moment of need, or when someone has the chance to crush us with shame, blame or humiliation, but instead chooses to love us, no matter our flaws, these are *love-energy* moments.

Love is more than a word, and the energy that flows between people informs our view on what love is. Where one person might experience how it feels to have the support of loving friends and family, another person might have experiences of limited support or no one to turn to. The more *love-energy* we experience the more expansive our knowledge of what love is.

Love is a balance of self-regulation and co-regulation. Love is the transformative moment we are all living for, these love epiphanies are one of the greatest perks

---

[1] Johnson, Sue (2013). Love Sense: The Revolutionary New Science of Romantic Relationships. Little, Brown Spark.

of being human. Love sees us in our flawed state, and we learn to trust love's loving eyes.

Can you imagine if we all learned how to reprove others through the eyes of love? Or if we learnt that even when we are corrected, we are still loved in spite of all of our unchecked flaws? There is no need to hide what is wrong with us when we know we are included no matter what.

A part of understanding love is realizing true love does not love blindly. Love is listening, seeing, and knowing.

> Love does not say: *"Keep on self-destructing, I love you anyhow."*
>
> Love says: *"What's the story of you hurting yourself this way?"*
>
> Love says: *"It's safe to tell me the truth."*
>
> And when the truth is told, love is safe.
>
> Love says: *"We will figure a way out of this together."*

Love is about being heard, being seen, being known, and offering these same affections to others, as we are able. The ebbs and flow of giving and receiving love is a wobbly process. Sometimes we get it and sometimes we don't.

> Love says: *"Good on you for the moments where you have gotten it.*
>
> *Good on you for the moments where you let yourself get gotten."*

Then Love says: *"Don't worry about getting all the moments right all the time.*

Be with people when you can as you can, be with yourself, when you can as you can."

I will tell you this. At times, I have acted in unloving ways to myself and to others. I have hurt people. Simply because I am a person just like everybody else. Sometimes I am good, and sometimes I am not. Sometimes I believe the lies my fear tells me, and sometimes I see and overcome such lies. Sometimes I wallow in my version of *"I belong alone,"* defaulting hard and bad and deep, and sometimes I take a breath and remind myself that I am loved, loveable and loving, just the way I am. You can understand this about me because you know this about you. We all have our own moments.

I am a person. You are a person. We are people who do not have to get it right all the time.

We are all people rescued by love,

Rescued by the epiphanies of love we have known.

Rescued by our hope for continued love epiphanies.

Rescued and rescued and rescued again.

Always rescued.

Because we are always accepted as whole people.

We are always included by Love.

We are always included in a love like this.

The human experience is filled with many *love-energy* moments, not one sole moment. Life is saturated with an abundance of resounding love. We all have *love-energy* moments in our relationships, and we can learn to see them.

> As we take the time to witness love, we know love, and love nudges us to know we are utterly included in the same heart of love as everyone else.

There is something healing about our human experience being imperfect. There is no possibility of getting it all right. We are imperfect. We are vulnerable to our imperfections, yet we are loved, and loveable, and loving.

> What does love do? Love keeps loving us without inquiring whether we deserve to be loved.

Contemplative question:

What do you say love is?

I am a psychologist by trade, so it is not a far stretch that I am writing a book about love. But some readers may be wondering just how much focus will be placed on God. As my understanding of attachment theory has grown, and as my experiences with people reinforced the science of love to my mind, I find myself continually wondering about where and how God fits in with *love-energy*. Allow me to take a few pages to clarify.

A WORD ABOUT G-O-D

Love never dies. Inspired speech will be over some day; praying in tongues will end; understanding will reach its limit. We know only a portion of the truth, and what we say about God is always incomplete. But when the Complete arrives, our incompletes will be canceled.
1 Corinthians 13:8-10, The Message[1]

I do not need to evangelize to anyone about any of their relationships. All of our relationships are complicated. I will not preach to you about having perfect relationships with yourself, with other people, or with God— quite the opposite.

Some of us will be uncomfortable about the exploration of *self-love*. Some will be challenged by our relationships with other people. Others will be frustrated to consider how a relationship with God is possible. All of this discomfort is understandable. We are contemplating love, after all. There is space for exploration and space to organize whatever comes along with it.[2] We are included as whole people. Likewise, we will consider how our whole self has experienced rejection in our relationship with ourselves, with others, and with God, as well as to honor and notice the ways we give and receive love.

---

[1] Peterson, Eugene H. (1993). *The Message: The Bible in Contemporary Language.* NavPress.

[2] Johnson, Sue. (2008). *Hold Me Tight: Seven Conversations for a Lifetime of Love.* Little, Brown Spark.

I do not hide my love of theology. What drew me to theology is a bit of an odd story. When I graduated high school, I wanted to go to a certain bible school because my friends were going. I also felt like I was good at thinking about God. I didn't know it at the time but looking back on many funny stories of odd comments I made in my adolescent and college years, I now realize I was actually good at questioning theories about God. I made a major life decision. I plunged into academia. Youthfulness and curiosity drove this choice point, and not much more.

After setting off to attend bible school in Caronport, Saskatchewan, Canada, I looked through the catalog of college degree descriptions. The one titled "Bachelors of Art in Theology" sounded smart, so I enrolled. I am not sure when I looked up the meaning of theology, but I do remember going to the college library and opening the big dictionary. There I found the definition: "theology: the study of God." I was fine with this revelation. I discovered the title I was pursuing. A very ordinary, naive, not that magically life determination, and definitely worth a chuckle. I am glad it worked out for me! Nonetheless, I have no regrets.

I do revel in thoughts of God. I enjoy thinking about God because I enjoy asking questions. I have made peace with this. I don't have many answers, a few, but not many. This fits with my theology practice. I have questions and I am okay to sit with these questions.

I assure you I have a nonevangelical nature. In this book I share my curiosity on how God and love go together, that's it. *Love-energy* and *Love's Energy.* A beautiful mystery.

If you have endured spiritual abuse, I hope there is enough safety in this book, in *Love's Energy,* for you to hold God lightly, as I trust God holds you lightly. If you do not believe in God, this is not a problem. It is also not a problem if you have lost belief in yourself, or if you have lost belief in humanity. You don't have to fit any certain mold to participate in this curious unravelling of love.

I do hope you will read the parts about God; I also hope those who do not have children will read the parts about parents, with openness and curiosity. I hope you will read all of the parts of this book, the parts that inspire you and the parts that challenge you— when you can, as you can.

| And don't forget to breathe.

This book falls into four sections titled: Loved, Lovable, and Loving, with a final section about Supernatural Love, titled *Love's Energy.* As we continue to understand our own nature, we will also unpack the science and the relational proof for our loved, lovable, and loving design. I don't want to divulge all the mystery of how *"who we are"* in our personhood draws us to wonder about the vast love we are all connected to. I also do not want to ply you with answers and solutions. My great hope is that you will find space to be refreshed, to be informed, and to be curious about your own self, and how you have your own unique place of belonging in the same heart of love as everyone else.

We are all so very loved. It is alright to doubt this. But the nature of our personhood revels in how loved, loveable and loving we are. So, let's begin right here.

Love and Love's Energy

Tara Boothby

LOVED

Love and Love's Energy

BEING HUMAN

"The most common form of despair is not being who you are." —Kierkegaard[1]

We are people like everyone else, sometimes we are good and sometimes we are bad. But we are always people, just like everybody else.

Over the next several chapters, we will spend time discovering, and rediscovering, our *being human*. Some of this information you will already know, and other information will be fresh —new. In order to make space for love that cherishes our value as individual people, love that abounds for us as whole people, love that includes us, we must begin by uncovering why we doubt love to begin with.

| Discovering *love-energy* is an inside job.

---

[1] Kierkegaard, Soren (1849). The Sickness unto Death. Penguin Classics.

Love and Love's Energy

YOUR SIDE OF THE STREET

"Remember also that you don't always need words to communicate understanding. Your willingness to sit quietly with a child as the two of you grapple with feelings speaks volumes. For one, it can indicate to your child that you take the matter seriously. It can also say that you agree that this is not an insignificant problem; it requires thought and attention. As you sit together with an emotion, know that a hug or a back rub often says more than words—especially if the child is grappling with sadness or fear."
John M. Gottman[1]

I have great respect for the Alcoholics Anonymous (AA) program. In the early years of my career, I worked as a clinical addiction counsellor, then later on I participated in the Celebrate Recovery Step Study. 12 step programs are well organized, inspiring, and from this culture comes the metaphor, *"clean up your side of the street."*[2] Maybe you have heard this phrase before.

> When I think of cleaning up my side of the street, I imagine a small-town street with two sides, each side with a sidewalk on their side of the roadway. I imagine walking down my side of the street, feeling the fresh air and the sunlight on me. In my mind's eye, I am rarely cleaning. I am more

---

[1] Gottman, John (1997). *Raising An Emotionally Intelligent Child: The Heart of Parenting.* Simon & Schuster.

[2] Alcoholics Anonymous World Services, Inc. (1989). *Twelve Steps and Twelve Traditions.* Alcoholics Anonymous World Services.

experiencing and enjoying my clean side of the street. I am not peeking over to see how the other side of the street looks, I am living on my side. It is as if I have already done the clean-up for that day. As if in the memory of the image, I remember having cleaned my side. I think this is because, in my experience, the cleaning happens in my day-to-day noticing and self-actualizing. Or maybe, the image allows me to remain hopeful that I can experience a clean side of my street, even though I am always a bit of a mess, never completely cleaned up.

What image comes to mind for you?

What does your side of the street look like?

There is no need to judge how your image is similar or different from mine. Take time to notice your unique image. Then consider jotting your image down somewhere.

Not only do we have our very own side of the street, but all the potency of our attachment fear and yearnings are the brick and mortar of the real-estate on our street. The sidewalk we walk down in our mind's eye is adjacent to our property. Our real-estate is the brick and mortar of all the stuff that makes up who we are: our view of ourselves, our view of other people, our history, and so on. Our real-estate is built completely by the life we have lived and the relationships we have had, good and bad.

> As I already mentioned, in my mind's eye, I view my side of the street as clean. But just earlier today I had a flood of emotion. In full disclosure, I can be riddled with sharp anxiety. All-at-once, I lost my footing, no one may have known, but my

inside world felt upside down. My side of the street, my real-estate, became unsafe, and a place I did not want to know.

How does the clutter of anxiety impact me? I used to chew my nails. I struggle with perfectionism. I am prone to plummeting self-loathing. At these times I often avoid people. All at once, I can fall into a negative view of myself and the world around me. I am better at digging myself out of these times (I'd like to call them moments, but they never feel short lived when they are my presence) and although I am better at helping myself cope when my inner world feels upside down, I still get triggered by what is happening in my present circumstances. Something happens, big or small, in my day, and the clutter of my side of my street takes over. My history, my negative thoughts, my flaws, can feel piled up and powerful. For me this presents as anxiety.

You and I are not very different. When the big gusts of emotional wind blow through our minds the clutter of bad habits, uncontrolled emotions, automatic negative thoughts, and so on, will cause disarray on your side of the street as much as on my side.

Our parents hold the original deed to our real-estate, as we hold the original deed to our children's real-estate. We become aware of our side of the street early in life, taking over the deed to our identity at a very early age, usually before we are developmentally ready to do so. As we become aware of our mess inside, we become more aware of our side of the street — our *inner working model* as attachment theorist John Bowlby calls it. This internal model informs our view of self, view of others, and view of the world around us, how we will respond to ourselves, others, and God.[1] The thing about our inner working model is that when we start to pay attention to who we are and how we are, we can choose to clean up some of our stuff, to self-actualize. We really have to see our mess to work with our mess.

> *"The thing about our inner working model is that it is always working."* —Jim Furrow[2]

When my inner working model is riddled with anxiety the landscape of my side of the street does not look or feel safe. When I do not feel at peace in my inner world. Of course, my view of self, view of others, and view of God is impacted. The less safe our inner world is, the less ability we have to see the world as safe for ourselves and others.

Our internal working model is informed by our early life experience. There are many groups of people who care about childhood attachment wounds and neglect. One group developed a questionnaire called ACE, the Adverse Childhood Experience Study.[3] Higher scores indicate you have had more adverse experiences in your family of origin therefore you are more at risk for later life problems. This questionnaire is simple yet powerful. It highlights a truth that has been backed up by research for years: When our natural tendency to trust our primary caregiver is disrupted, this disruption puts us at risk of making bad decisions, acting out in unsafe ways, creating a system of defaults to protect

---

[1] Brentherton I. (1992). *The Origins of Attachment Theory: John Bowlby and Mary Ainsworth.* Developmental Psychology, 63(6): 1456-1472.

[2] Verbal communication EFFT workshop (2023), Canmore, Alberta.

[3] Felitti, Anda, Nordenberg, Williamson, Spitz, Edwards, Marks. (1998). *Relationship of Childhood Abuse and Household Dysfunction to Many of the Leading Causes of Death in Adults: The Adverse Childhood Experience (ACE) Study.* American Journal of Preventive Medicine 14(4), 245-258.

ourselves from the pain of being outside of the relationships we were born to experience.[1] The more adversity we have faced the greater the likelihood we will act with adversity in our relationships. Adversity influences our internal working model and clutters our side of the street.

> The more adversity a child experiences the less safe their inner world. This impacts their inner real-estate; this influences their inner working model.

It is hard to live with the messiness of being human. The more mess we have experienced in our life, the more we want to avoid looking at our mess. Thus, the less likely we are to clean up our side of the street, quite probably the less likely we are to believe we have capacity to be clean on the inside, or even know how to begin to clean up our inner world.

This is sad. The more disruption a child experiences in their early primary relationships the messier a child sees themselves, the more flawed they feel. Such a child is more likely to hide away, to live with fear and reinforce their belief — *"I belong alone."* The more trauma a child endures, the more potential that they will continue to live in trauma, look for, act out, self-sabotage, succumb, to believe they are a mess. All of this, all the garbage and debris which will clutter this child's side of the street.

> Because the real-estate purchase that was made for us has a huge influence on our side of the street, the brick and mortar, our sidewalk, all the fractures and neglect, the rot, the worries, the flaws and fear, all impact our ability to clean up.

---

[1] Felitti, et al.

When parents themselves are the product of abuse and neglect, it is extremely hard to break the only cycle they have ever known. How heartbreaking for a parent to have the initial experience of laying their loving eyes on their brand-new miracle, then to have their ability to cultivate love erode. Parenting is hard. Parenting is even harder when we have our own trauma story. It is true that many parents lose their ability to trust their own good intention, and many parents hurt their children in big and small ways.[1] Even good parents cause damage.

I'll say it again here: some people make grave mistakes in caring for children. Earth shattering things happen to many young people behind closed doors, this is never okay. If you are a survivor of childhood abuse and neglect, I wish I could sit with you and hear your story. I wish I could slow down with you, to be present with you, to keep pace with you, to get to know you. I wish I could hear you and let you feel heard and seen. I know there are other people who feel this exact way about you. You may not have met any of us yet, but you can.

If you have not had an opportunity to share your pain story, please find a people helper who you feel safe with. Then go as slow as you need to with your words. But start to speak.

| You deserve to be heard, and seen, and known.

Our family of origin relationships are complicated; therefore, it is normal to feel complicated feelings when we think about our childhood experiences. Your side of the street with your real-estate, is your story, whatever it may be. Your family of origin has impacted

---

[1] Furrow, James L., Palmer, Gail, Johnson, Sue M., Faller, George, Palmer-Olsen, Lisa (2019). *Emotionally Focused Family Therapy: Restoring Connection and Promoting Resilience*. Routledge.

you and your ability to take care of yourself and the people you love.

Trauma, neglect, abuse, loss — terrible things happen to people; terrible things happen to children who have no defense. If this resonates with you sit with your sadness:

Feel sad for yourself,

For your own experience.

Feel sad for your people,

For their experience. Feel sad for the little ones in your life,

How they have been hurt by others, how they have been hurt by you.

This is the cleaning up process.

We notice and we feel.

We learn to be present with our own story when we can, as we can.

Contemplative Questions:

What is the story of your side of the street?

What does knowing this story mean for you and what will you do with it?

Just now, what complicated feelings do you feel lurking?

Over the next several chapters, we will expand on our inner self: our defaults, our flaws, our fear, our version of *"I belong alone,"* as well as introduce our value: our *pure-of-heartness*.

Let's get rolling. Let's understand our inner working model.

DEFAULT STRATEGIES

"It has become apparent that the pattern of adjustment (over domains) is more significant for the understanding of the individual than any single measurement, or any total score."
Mary Ainsworth[1]

Our defaults are the ways we attempt to cover up what we perceive is undesirable about us. We strategize and try on different types of behaviors. The behaviors we evaluate as successful, the ones that we believe hide our flawed nature, we hold on to. The defaults which do not work we feel flawed for trying, and we work to omit such unsuccessful strategies from our repertoire. We hold on to certain strategies, we use them readily, we practice and perfect, and eventually these strategies become automatic. The more we use certain strategies the more automatic they become. These automatic strategies are our defaults.

> Our defaults can be defined as the image we present to the world to achieve the level of admiration we believe is tolerable for us.

Let's take a moment to consider people throughout history, after all history is full of examples of messy people. How many historic figures have obvious flaws of character? Even the Bible is a great example of tons of messy people who did many screwed up things and still made it into one of the longest standing historical

---

[1] Ainsworth (Salter), Mary, Blehar, Mary C., Waters, Everett, Wall, Sally (1979). *Patterns of Attachment: A Psychological Study of the Strange Situation.* Routledge.

texts, one of the most esteemed guidelines of moral living. How ironic is that?

> The most admirable people in the Bible, the Greek gods, historic figures, heroes of folklore, our favorite characters from classic fiction, are all messy and flawed.

The flawed characters of the bible really are fascinating. There are many sources of spiritual beliefs, and many ways people will use spiritual doctrines to shame us about our flawed nature. Yet the characters of such texts are flawed, as much as the authors of these writings are flawed in their nature. If we are meant to get everything perfect, follow the rules, then hide when we break such rules, then why are all of these flawed people included in the Bible?

The Bible includes illegitimate mothers, whores, rapists, murderers, dictators, liars, cowards, betrayers, deserters, alcohol abusers, white collar criminals, the marginalized, outcasts, sick, weak, rude, ruined, etc. All of which are included — all. The Bible includes many stories of people stepping outside the line and still being admired as being loved by God.

People in the Bible are both flawed and included. People throughout history are both flawed and included. Even if we decide to ignore the flawed person, their contribution cannot lose its impact. We can hide the flawed person from our mind's eye, but our mind cannot lose the merit of their contribution, try as we might.

We are not going to talk about the Bible beyond this example, but I think it is such a potent example of how we omit this necessary truth:

> People are flawed. People are messy. People are included.

We are flawed and loved. We are messy and included. In the very same way those who have gone before us have been flawed, messy, loved, loveable, loving, and included. And, just like those who have gone before us we are flawed, messy, loved, loveable, loving, perfectly-imperfect and included. We make mistakes. We repeat mistakes. We break the rules. We break the rules again. We have flaws, and our experience of being flawed, and then we interpret what we perceive are our flawed shortcomings. This becomes a pattern and keeps us stuck in loops of negative beliefs about ourselves and about other people.

Why do we try to shut our minds to our own flaws? Why do we hide our own flaws? Why do we contrive an image to present to the world just to hide our whole self? After all, we are all just people like everybody else, perfectly-imperfect. Being shamed for the parts of us we find shameful perpetuates our experience of being alone in the universe which further causes us to question our being included, naturally we then try to hide our flaws. We create methods to present ourselves as more desirable. We lose sight of the lineage we are included in, a history of whole people, not perfect people. We forget that history is full of examples of messy people. Messy like us.

We all struggle to trust we are okay. We know we are flawed on the inside, and so we invent an image in an attempt to cover our flaws. When we pay attention to this inventing and covering, we can see a pattern, we strategize until we settle on the defaults that work for our desired outcomes. We each do this in our unique way, but here are some examples of defaults:

> Types of default strategies: *over-functioning, under-functioning, perfectionism, self-sabotage, being tough, intelligence, addictions, self-harm, self-help, cold demeanor, humor, sarcasm, knowledge, spirituality, religion, judging, gossiping, slandering, codependency, caregiver-aholic, workaholic, clowning, neediness, power, success, fame, toxicity, narcissism, learned helplessness, histrionics, being charming, fake smiles, glam, faking good, flirting, filters, fillers, and more.* Do any of these words sound like you? Take note. Also take note of anything you would add that I have missed.

Our defaults are our invented method to present our desired image to the world around us, our effort to cover what we perceive is flawed about who we are.

Adding to the definition of our defaults, we also note that defaults are our go-to attachment strategy. How we strategize to either move into relationships, or to move away from relationships. This moving in or moving out of relationship is our attachment strategy; our default way of hiding our flaws in an effort to maintain some type relationships with others.[1]

> Years ago, I read The DNA of Relationships by Gary Smalley.[2] In his book, Smalley talked about how we write negative messages about who we believe we are on our hearts and how these messages influence our lives. I love this image.
>
> I conjured up a picture of how we have terrible things tattooed on our literal human hearts. Can you picture a human heart with words tattooed

---

[1] Bowlby, John. (1988). *A Secure Base: Parent-Child Attachment and Healthy Human Development.* Basic Books.

[2] Smalley, Gary, Smalley, Greg, Smalley, Michael, Paul, Robert (2007). *The DNA of Relationships.* Tyndale House Publishers, Inc.

on it? And, just now, as we consider how we use our defaults to cover our flaws, imagine how the message on our hearts influences our defaults.

How difficult it is to remove a tattoo. Keeping with this image, what is tattooed on your heart is your view of yourself. I have my tattoo on my heart, just as you do, just as everyone else does. This may be fine if we have positive truths permanently etched in our flesh, but what lies are tattooed on your heart? And what will it take to remove these lies about who you are and replace them with the truth?

One of the most jaw dropping things that happened when I read Smalley's book is that he had a list of what he called core fears. And on his list was the word *hypocrite*. Seeing that word and feeling all the fear I have associated with being a *hypocrite* was so profound for me. Prior to reading that list of fears, deep down I had always feared I was a *hypocrite*, I just did not know I was allowed to be afraid of being one.

My core fear says: *"I am a hypocrite, and I am afraid of being a hypocrite."* Saying this was a good first step for me. As I used Smalley's model and his list of fear words with clients, I would share my own fear word: *hypocrite*. I became acquainted with this word. I got good at saying my own fear out loud. I got good at hearing myself say: *"I am afraid I am a hypocrite."* I listened to myself. I started to see myself more fully, and included my fear of being a *hypocrite* as a part of who I am, not a secret fear. I began to see how when my inner fear went unchecked, I would act out in ways that I derived to protect myself but these methods of acting out would inevitably reinforce my fear. I became more aware of my inner fear, and I realized my defaults did not protect me in the ways I believed they would but rather, by avoiding my whole perfectly-imperfect self, the value of the tattoo on my heart: *hypocrite*.

Once I developed language for my internal fear, I could begin to see my defaults more clearly. There are many ways I personally default, but largely, when I make a mistake, I become very anxious, and if I do not notice my fear it can start to influence me. Eventually I will ruminate on what I did not do well, why I feel like a *hypocrite*, and I will get stuck in loops of *self-loathing*.

Self-loathing is not an easy default to see. Sometimes it may show up as sarcasm or self-depreciation, arrogance and performing; for me anyhow. My dominant default is to over function, at times I will refer to this as being a *workaholic*. My defaults get me very, very busy, to avoid whatever I perceive to be failure, whether that failure is something that has already happened or something I project may happen in the future. Failure is a key word associated with how I see myself as flawed, and over functioning is key to how I default to hide my flaws.

Not all fear is created equal. There is a good chance that my core fear is different from yours. Our fear about who we are are reinforced when we make mistakes and feel flawed. Then we strategize to cover our flaws. We feel afraid inside and we do something to help ourselves have some sense of balance in the world around us and our relationships. Whether we move in or move out of relationships, we are trying to find a method to be with people, to have love in our lives, at the level that we determine is tolerable for us. Some of us see relational distance will soothe us; while others see relational closeness will soothe us. Neither is better; they're merely different views. Whether we prefer to move in for relationship or prefer to move out, our attachment strategy is at the foundation of our defaults. Those who move in for emotional closeness will be more drawn to some types of defaults while those who move out for emotional distance will be more drawn to other types of defaults. Think cause and effect or how magnets work together.

> Listed here are ways *mover inners* tend to default to maintain relationship: *extroverted, people-pleasing, caregiving, full social calendar, being the center of attention, complain when others are busy, dramatic, friendship focused, playing the martyr, acting helpless, rallying their troops, criticizing, group think, needy of time, charming, seeking approval, overly loving, comforting, self-sacrificing, always aware of relational distance and closeness.* In attachment theory, mover inners could be referred to as people with anxious attachment.[1]

> Listed here are ways *mover outers* tend to default to maintain relationship: *self-sufficiency, cerebral, aloof, performance driven, hard time asking for help, relieved when others are busy, productive, results focused, private, guarded, trouble-shooting, fix it mentality, good at finding solutions, conflict avoidant, judgmental of errors, standoffish, efficient in communication, concise, self-scrutinizing, introverted, stonewalling, peacekeeping, placate, consistent, reliable, dependable, reasoning and*

---

[1] Hoffman, Kent, Copper, Glen, Powell, Bert (2017). *Raising a Secure Child: How Circle of Security Parenting Can Help You Nurture Your Child's Attachment, Emotional Resilience, and Freedom to Explore.* Guilford Press.

diffusing emotion. In attachment theory when we see people using clusters of these behaviors, we may use the term avoidant attachment.[1]

Most of us are drawn more to one or the other, *moving in* or *moving out of relationships*. If you are someone who moves both in and out, don't worry. We all have the capacity to move in at times and out at other times. We all have our own unique mix, and rarely does anyone fit purely in one category.

We cannot definitively say defaults are bad. Our defaults are our strategy for living. As such, most of us cultivate a presence in the world to keep our flaws hidden, we usually do not want to call negative attention to ourselves so we choose defaults that will meet our need for relational closeness and distance in a method that will not cause complete social disaster. Remember: defaults are not all created equal. Some hurt us. Often though, they do not hurt us at all, many times our defaults seem to benefit us:

The funny guy gets people laughing. The pretty girl gets people looking. The thinking person gets people thinking. The argumentative person gets people riled up. The religious person gets to feel a sense of control. The caregiver gets to keep people close. The loner gets to stay safe. The performer gets to be admired. The rebel gets people wondering about them. The partier gets invited to the party. The gossip gets to be the center of attention. The bully is saved from more pain. The eccentric stays hidden. The perfectionist feels powerful, and so on. Each person grabs a way of being in the world and keeps practicing it until it is as natural to them as skin. After all, if our defaults do not get some good results why would we keep using them? The risk is when we have an automatic way of being. Even if we get some desired outcomes anything

[1] Clinton, Tim, Sibcy, Gary (2009). *Attachments: Why You Love, Feel, and Act the Way You Do.* Thomas Nelson.

automatic always has associated risks. When is it ever good to shut off our brain and trust autopilot?

When we put our personhood on auto and we live without thought, we are disconnected from our whole self. The more our defaults become automatic, the more *alone* we will feel on the inside. We may have a life benefitted by the results of our defaults, yet we will not be living in the fullness of who we are.

> The detriment of defaults happens when they become automatic because when we are living on autopilot we have limited access to our authentic whole self, we have limited awareness of our inner world, our emotions, thoughts, and decision making. Our flaws may remain hidden, but at what cost?

In my personal story, earlier in this chapter, I shared how I began to notice my inner fear of being a hypocrite. This word is associated with my inner loneliness. Naming my fear and talking about it was my first step. As I spoke about my fear more I could see the times I was strategizing to cover my fear, to hide my flaws. I began to notice my defaults more and more. I became a noticer of the false persona I was putting out. I named my fear and then I began to observe myself more and more. I am not perfect at this, I still hit autopilot from time to time, just like everyone else. The goal is to notice how our inner fear gets us defaulting to hide what we are afraid is flawed about ourselves.May we learn to become noticers.

May we notice our whole selves.

May we notice what we do that causes us harm.

*May we notice what we do that affords us help.
May we ponder until we believe in the value of being whole people.May we notice love and*

May we wonder more about the energy of love.

Contemplation Questions:

What defaults do you see yourself submitting to?

How do these defaults impact your life?

How do these defaults impact your relationships?

Love is a wonderful healing force to help us heal our defaults. *Love-energy* gives us powerful hope for ourselves and our relationships. But to truly understand love we also need to hold space to discuss the pain we carry inside. Loneliness is a common dilemma.

I BELONG ALONE

"Perhaps the inner motive is that the fact of being loved disinterestedly reminds us that we all need love from others and depend upon the charity of others to carry on our own lives. And we refuse love, and reject society, in so far as it seems, in our own perverse imagination, to imply some obscure kind of humiliation."
Thomas Merton[1]

Merton shares this philosophy in his autobiography after he tells the story of his boyhood cruelty to his younger brother. He has a vivid memory of throwing stones at his brother and seeing the emotional pain his brother has. He notes his brother longs to be with him even though Merton is being cruel. He tells of his own mixed feelings between his cruel attitude and his awareness of his brother's hope and hurt. We all have a story like this one, as the bully or as the outcast. It is common to try on an image of *disinterested love*. Maybe we call it indifference, or aloofness, or at times, clear rejection of others.

To offer disinterest is unloving.

To receive disinterest is to feel unloved.

Neither are experiences of love at all.

What Merton labels disinterested love can be noticed in moments where we feel alone. Times we are not met, and we really need someone to meet us. All the stories where we feel unmeetable. We bank these stories as proof that we are unworthy of love, that we

[1] Merton, Thomas (1948). *The Seven Storey Mountain.* Harcourt, Inc.

are destined to be alone. I call this pile-up of painful disinterests our "I belong alone." It is common to us all, even though it shows up in a variety of different ways, the core is the same.

> Here are examples of versions of *"I belong alone"* that drive our defaults:
>
> *I am lonely. I am isolated. I am outside. I am abandoned. I am a liar. I am a fraud. I am neglected. I am abused. I am lost. I am punished. I am a hypocrite. I am heartless. I am empty. I am defective. I am inadequate. I am broken. I am scared. I am a burden. I am betrayed. I am vile. I am too much. I am too little. I am already condemned. I am hopeless. I am helpless. I am on my own. I am invisible. I am denied. I am robbed. I am hated. I am violent. I ruin everything. I love people more than they love me. I give and get nothing. I don't fit in. I am dead inside. I am not wanted. No one will notice when I am gone. I am better off dead. I am fucked up.*

Can you see words on this list that are familiar to the painful places you hide deep inside?

Do you have a sense of your version of *"I belong alone"*?

Take all the time you need to note the words that sound true for you, or to consider your own words. Hopefully sharing some of the language I have used, or heard others use in my office, will inspire you to feel into the experience of your *"I belong alone."* As I've mentioned, we are all flawed creatures, and we know it. We believe this is the root cause of our loneliness. Then, we strategize to cover our flaws and fear. We practice our defaults, refine our defaults, get excellent at our defaults, to hide our version of *"I belong alone"* because we struggle to believe our whole self will be accepted.

> We all have an *"I belong alone"* narrative — unique words, stories, proof we collect to go along with our version of "I belong alone." Do you know the details of your narrative?

Feeling lonely then being afraid is normal. Hiding our fear is also normal. We hide our fear about the love we have not been included in. Or rather, we hide our fear about the love we perceive we have not been included in. When we believe we are alone we look for proof we are not included, as we find *proof,* we create our narrative to suit. This leads us to believe we will never be included, at least not if people realize how flawed we are. Our lonely narrative fuels our default way of hiding our flaws. To protect us from the risks of our mess being divulged. This is a common human experience though it feels completely unique. Afterall, we all yearn for love.

Love is an energy experience.

Unique to each of us.

Common to all of us.

At our most troubling times we are afraid to be exposed as *"who I really am"*. We are afraid of what might happen if others see *"who I really am."* We believe the narrative our *"alone"* defines us by.

> When I share my version of *"I belong alone,"* people are often surprised that my *"alone"* fear is the fear I am a *heartless* person. If you look at my life as a devout psychologist, as a person who builds up mental health workers, and hear me speak about love and attachment, then knowing I

worry about being *heartless* is shocking. I get it. I have even had wise attachment leaders say to me, *"you don't believe that."* What a terrible response. On some level, I do believe it. And, when I hurt myself or other people hurt me, when I hurt others, there will always be a part of me afraid *I am alone* in my pain moment because *I am heartless*. I no longer deny this fear, nor do I believe it is true, but there are still moments for me where fear takes over, this is why it is so good to know what I am afraid of.

These days, I feel sad for myself about the lonely narrative I have. Learning to be open helps. I open up to myself about myself and my flaws and see my defaults for what they are. I catch myself when my negative perceptions start to pile up, when my narrative starts to get dramatic. Sure, I still feel pain when *"I am alone"* moments happen for me and I still wonder if all my worst perceptions about myself are true (or will come true), but I do this less and less. The greatest source of healing my lonely narrative is knowing all of the parts of who I am are loved, lovable and loving.

It is okay to fear we will end up banished to our aloneness. We take our version of *"I belong alone"* with us, as well as our fear. We get to be whole people. Whole people who worry about being alone, because being alone is unnatural to our nature and our nurture.

It does continue to surprise me how my narrative has less and less influence as I work through accepting that I am truly loved, loveable, and loving. My fear of being *heartless* is less potent, and I have more trust in my *pure-of-heartness*.

From a fear of being *heartless* to trusting my *pure-of-heartness* is a transformation I continue to work on. But what a transformation!

Do you know you are *pure-of-heart*?

I have come to a point in my life where I have tamed my fear of being *heartless* by learning to love my fear and take it with me on life's journey. This makes room for a greater acceptance of my *pure-of-heartness* and the beauty of trusting how completely included I am. I accept that I am loved and accepted just the way I am. Even though I am still afraid at times that I am *heartless*, or that others will expose me as *heartless*, I trust I am included in the same heart of love as everyone else. This beautiful trust helps me make room for my flaws, and my afraid, worried, alone inner places. This same trust allows me to love me and carry all my darkness and flaws with me on my road to being a whole and authentic person.

> *Again, it's important to remember that the worry, the fear, and our individual version of alone stays with us forever –wholeness is not defined by a lack of faults or fear, instead we are now learning that every bit of who we are is covered by love, and every bit of who we are is included - We are whole people.*
>
> *We are wholly loved.*
>
> *We are wholly unshunned.*

Shutting our eyes does not make scary things go away. Turning away from our aloneness does not make us less alone. Seeing ourselves as we are — flaws, fear, and beauty — is transformative. So, my friends, alone is a secret best spoken.

Let your fear be heard.

Let it be visualized. Let it be known.

If we want to start the process of discovering our whole self, it is good to reach out and ask for someone else to be with us as we expose and unravel these places. At first, this unraveling may be painful. It is often a vulnerable experience riddled with anxiety and fear, and almost always tears (sometimes, though, tears become the best part). But this is a beautiful unraveling, a shedding of what we have done to ourselves by trying to keep our mess all to ourselves. We have lived our version of *"I belong alone"* for far too long.

We can do some of this healing on our own, but we also need other people with us in this process. We are here to experience *love-energy* and having at least one other human for this unraveling will soothe our alone place. Then, when we start to unravel our own *pure-of-heartness*, we also discover how our moving in and out of relationships can be more emotionally safe.

The goal is to have a renewed relationship with ourselves and with others. In this fresh experience of our deepened, deeply satisfying relationships we will experience the fullness of what we are created to be with other people, moments of epiphany, of resounding in these relationships, soothing and comforting our version of *"I belong alone."*

> Being afraid we are destined to be alone will never change the truth that we are included in the same heart of love as everyone else.

Contemplative Questions:

What is your version of *"I belong alone?"*

What perceptions and stories inform your lonely narrative?

Before we go on, I want to say one thing very clearly: your identity matters. You! The way you are! You! I am not saying this to gush. I am saying this as a fact.

> May you have a renewed and deepened sense of your own value. May your definition of love be shaken and revived. May you know you are loved and valued no matter your mess. May your *pure-of-heart* nature be revealed to you.

We have begun to see how our *"I belong alone"* narrative takes root for each of us, let's keep on this journey to discover how our story uniquely develops and expands with personal complexity.

Love and Love's Energy

OUR FEAR

People often come to see a psychologist when they notice their default persona is causing them pain. Psychological healing begins when someone learns to dive under their skin in search of themselves, and discovers how to love themselves as they are, flaws and all, and to see their *"I belong alone"* not as true, but as a manifestation of their fear—fear which is also loved.

At times, I sit with teenagers who have to divulge a secret to their parents. I have learned the moment the secret hits the air, there is a sense of relief… for at least a moment. And then, if the parents let themselves hear their child's courage and fear rather than focus on the flaws of this divulged secret they have just heard, *love-energy* shows up. The teen feels known in a new way. This is very similar to what it is like for us as we begin to dive into and then share our inner world with ourselves and others. It is frightening to start, but it can lead to relief and healing.

It doesn't always work this way. When we are the listener, sometimes we need help to hear someone else as they share their pain with us. We get frightened by people sharing their flaws because we are frightened by our own flaws. We are afraid to speak about our flaws. We are afraid to hear others' flaws.

> I assure you the most awful things are not what you think they will be.

Sharing your flaws, recovering your lonely story, being mindful of your defaults will not be the experience you fear it will be.

If you are not sure how to be safe, or who to be safe with, you are not the only one. If you are out of practice at being in a safe relationship or trusting your instincts about people, start with a therapist.

You will cultivate safe relationships. Hold curiosity for love and you will discover proof of *love-energy*.

Contemplative Questions:

What does fear have you believing about yourself and other people?

What does fear get you believing is flawed about you?

What does fear get you doing? How are you living in the world around you to hide your fears and flaws? How does your default persona show up?

It is never lost on me just how heavy some of the process of self-discovery can feel. Do you feel heavy after these last two chapters? If your heart is heavy take space to take care of yourself. I am hopeful the next chapter will help to lighten whatever complicated feelings may be stirring.

PURE-OF-HEART

I was born in a small town in northern Alberta. Two weeks after I was born, we moved from that town, and I have never returned. I rarely run into anyone who resides there. A few years back, I stumbled onto the teachings of William Paul Young, the author of *The Shack*, and a super cool theologian.[1] He is very transparent with his personal story of his flaws and his beliefs about God's inclusive love. In one of his testimonies, I heard him say: "I was born in Grand Prairie, Alberta." I couldn't believe it. He was the first person I knowingly had a connection to that was born in the same town as I.

At the time, Paul was co-facilitating a theology class I was participating in. This connection afforded me an opportunity to build a friendship with Paul. I am forever grateful for the hours he has spent with me as a person. When I zoom out and look at the big picture, Paul has always spent time with me for no other reason than the reason I exist. This gesture, that Paul gives of his time with expectation in return, causes me to confront some parts of who I am.

At one point, Paul said to me, "You know you're *pure-of-heart*, right? What obliterated my [default] was when I realized my *pure-of-heartness*!" This comment sticks with me even

---

[1] Young, William Paul (2007). *The Shack: Where Tragedy Confronts Eternity.* Windblown Media, Faithwords, Hodder & Stoughton.

now. This comment plays over and over in my mind and swims through every corner of who I am. Up until I met Paul, the potency of a *pure-of-heart* identity was lost to me.

I rehearsed Paul's words in my mind for a long time: "What obliterated my [default] was when I realized my pure-of-heartness!" I sat with the discomfort of not knowing how to believe those words were true for me, and at the same time I trusted Paul seemed to have something I didn't. At that moment of realization, I saw Paul accepted his flaws and loved even the worst parts of who he was. He believed somehow that his whole self was loved in a grander spiritual sense. He believed in God, he had an exhaustive knowledge of Jesus, and he had a different sense of trusting he was loved by God—flaws and all.

| Loved, flaws and all, and still pure-of-heart.

I can't say for certain the moment when these words made their home in me. I will say what has obliterated my fear of being *heartless* is I now recognize my *pure-of-heartness*. Accepting that I am *pure-of-heart* also helps me cope and remedy my defaults. I am less hypervigilant, I am less controlling of myself and the outcomes I thought I controlled, I realize I am not responsible to solve every problem that I am presented with. Now when I screw up, because I often do, my *pure-of-heartness* is vital to me loving my flaws and soothing my personal narrative of *"I belong alone"*. I am now able to drop my defaults more often, and like Paul, I have had the same obliteration of my fear and some of my most intense defaults.

What I ask of you is to take this question with you: *"You know you're pure-of-heart, right?"* Take it with you. Let it percolate inside of you. Let yourself wonder about how it fits, or does not fit, with your version of *"I belong alone."* Begin to wonder what your *pure-of-heartness* might *obliterate* in your life. If you want to devote time daily, or even weekly, to wrestle with this question, great. Of all the things you will read in this book, I hope this is one you will not turn the page and forget.

You were born with a pure heart.

Your pure heart is the true nature of who you are.

Your pure-of-heartness will sooth all of the parts of who you are,

Your pure-of-heartness will help you know that you are included,

Just the way you are,

In the same heart of love as everyone else,

Where you will always be included.

Contemplative Questions:

You Know you are pure of heart, right?

Take a moment for this to wash over you.

There is a good chance I am challenging your beliefs about yourself and the world around you. Are you finding yourself challenged to shift your thinking on love and people? The shifting is hopeful, albeit unpleasant at times. Life is a process of taking in new information and learning how to grow and change with what we are learning. We make meaning from the good and bad times in our lives. Let's take some time to refresh on the importance of making meaning from the circumstances of our lives; let's take some time to reflect on existentialism.

EXISTENTIAL CRISIS, SHIFTS, & EPIPHANY

"No one man can become fully aware of the very essence of another human being unless he loves him."
Viktor Frankl[1]

"Each man is questioned by life; and he can only answer to life by answering for his own life."
Viktor Frankl[2]

Existential crises are moments of epiphany which present us with a life-changing challenge. These moments challenge us to consider if we are willing to let go and transform our view of who we are, how we see the world around us, and what we believe is the meaning of life.?"[3]

It takes courage to sit on the therapy couch and confess your fallibility to an expert. Of course, many people worry they are a hopeless case. It is scary business to confess your shortcomings. It makes sense that in every one of these brave moments of confession, the people in my office must have a glimmer of fear. They must worry I will tell them they are a lost cause.

We are failures if we break... or so we think. Viktor Frankl, famously associated with existentialism, was working on his questions about the

---

[1] Frankl, Viktor E. (1959) *Man's Searching For Meaning.* Beacon Press.
[2] Frankl, Viktor E. (1959) *Man's Searching For Meaning.* Beacon Press.
[3] Kierkegaard, Soren (1849). *The Sickness Unto Death: A Christian Psychological Exposition of Edification & Awakening by Anti-Climacus.* Penguin Classics.

meaning of life when he was taken captive during the Holocaust. He walked into the evil of the concentration camp armed with his belief: *"Bad things happen, and we make meaning from them.[1]* Viktor writes of how he and other prisoners survived, while millions died. He believed he needed to feel the pain and uncertainty of all the dire moments in his life and make meaning from his pain as much as he made meaning from the joys he experienced. He was placed in unthinkable torture and still made meaning from it.

I find it fascinating he already had his theories about existential shifts and meaning written prior to his concentration camp imprisonment. He carried them in his jacket pocket. He had already learned to have a loving mind toward his suffering. I am certain he wondered many times if he would be alive at the end of World War II. But armed with his beliefs about meaning, he was better able to turn his loving mind toward himself. He could hear himself with loving ears, see himself with loving eyes, and make meaning of who he was. Viktor advocated that looking for meaning in whatever circumstances we face helps us to maintain hope for our own personhood.

> Existential crises are powerful because they lead to existential shifts, when we are willing.[2]

Frankl could not survive his concentration camp experience without being changed by his experience. He decided he needed to make meaning from it. Like Frankl, existential crises challenge us to change as people or to return to our homeostasis, that which we have always known—our comfort zone. When we stay in our homeostasis, we run the risk of always going back to what is comfortable for us, and

---

[1] Frankl, Viktor E. (1959) *Man's Searching For Meaning*. Beacon Press.
[2] Marcel, Gabriel (1956). *The Philosophy of Existentialism*. Citadel Press.

consequentially, we stop ourselves from asking questions about who we are. When we do not question ourselves, we risk suffering and not discovering meaning. We risk staying the same.

The thing about existential crises is most of the time they are not war camp moments. Many meaningful moments constantly present themselves over the span of our lives. Some are big, like war, or the pandemic lockdowns. Smaller ones happen almost daily in an ongoing way:

The developmental milestones of infants and small children, going to school each year as a child and adolescent, learning to read, puberty, not fitting in, failure, adolescent independence, identity formation, injuries, losing friends, choosing an adult life path, going to university, learning to pay bills, learning to carry debt, falling in love, getting our hearts broken, deciding to marry, getting married, having children, getting fired, bad investments, changing careers, battling illness, having people we love get ill, having people we love die, our parent's dying, divorce, retirement, our bodies aging, our peers dying, the violence of the world, the world continuing to advance, and more. All of these are normal, all are existential crises or shifts.As we experience times of crisis, we will continue to have moments where we are challenged to hear ourselves with loving ears, see ourselves with loving eyes, and know ourselves with a loving mind. And to question ourselves:

Why do I do the things I do? Are my thoughts serving me? Are my behaviors serving me? What meaning do I make from the bad that happens in my life? How do I allow myself to participate in relationships? Do I admit my mistakes? How do I use and misuse trust? In what way am I existing? Why am I existing this way? What is the purpose of existence if I am hiding my whole self behind my defaults? Why do I exist?

How beautiful it will be for us to put love at the heart of meaning making. We make meaning from our suffering, and we discover Love. Love is at the heart of our existence because we are all included in the same heart of love. Love carries valuable influence over the meaning that we make, if we allow it to.

> *The nature of love ascribes meaning for our very existence. Living with meaning assures us we are designed by love,*
>
> *Included by love, &*
>
> *Existing within love.*

Contemplative Questions:

What is the meaning of your life?

What is the purpose of your life?

How does love help or hinder your meaning making? We all have times where we discover more hope for our lives, and we all have times where we see we have been left unresolved by hardship. As Frankl suggests, we must learn to choose how we respond to the very low times of our lives as well as the very good times. Choosing how to respond to life is powerful, and it is the focus of our next chapter.

YOU GET TO CHOOSE WHO YOU ARE IN ALL OF YOUR RELATIONSHIPS

> *"Out there things can happen, and frequently do,*
> *To people as brainy and footsy as you.*
> *And when things start to happen, don't worry, don't stew.*
> *Just go right along, you'll start happening too!"*
> Dr. Seuss[1]

One of my go-to lines with people when they are struggling in relationships is this:

> "You get to choose who you are in all of your relationships."

When we touch our hurt relationships and pay attention, it is natural for us to feel afraid we will be caught in our misbehavior. In these times it is easy to forget:

> We have a choice about who we are and how we are in the world around us.

We have freedom to choose to enjoy our relationship with ourselves—to participate in *self-love*. This participation is riddled with hope and peace and moments of breaking through the existential dilemmas we discussed in the last chapter.

---

[1] Seuss, Dr. (1990). *Oh, The Places You'll Go!* Random House Books For Young Readers.

No matter what your story is, no matter your past, no matter your current circumstance, you get to choose who you are in all of your relationships, regardless of your relationships. The flip side is also true, you have been deciding who you are. We all are always deciding who we are, though we rarely pay attention to these decisions (remember our early discussion about defaults and autopilot). The good news is that at this very moment we can start to pay attention.

At times, life is unkind to us. For some, life is very, very unkind. We still have a choice. Not noticing our power of choice is a decision in itself. In the past we may have believed we were powerless. We may have believed we had no other option of how to be with people. But here we are, learning something new. We are learning how to unleash our capacity to be mindful about choosing who we are in our relationships based on who we want to be in our relationships. We are allowing space for our own curiosity about our whole self.

> You get to choose who you are in all of your relationships.

You get to like who you are in all of your relationships. It is okay to doubt this, to be troubled to believe how likeable you actually are. Take a pause and wrestle this one through if need be. There is no requirement to embrace everything you are learning about *love-energy*. We are learning to ask questions, to lean into life in a new way. Within this new way there is space to percolate, to disagree, to say, *"I'm not sure about this one."*

When we do not see our ability to choose who we are, we often end up living in a state of sacrifice. We sacrifice ourselves over and over for our perceived limits or for the limits we perceive in other people. We have a tough time believing it is possible to like ourselves in all of our relationships, or any of our relationships, least of all our relationship with ourselves. But all is not lost when we learn to take hold of our choices about who we are.

Business relationships are not easy. I can conjure up many personal examples of times I have chosen well just as much as I can recall times I have chosen poorly. It is easy for me to mismanage my emotions when I am trying to remain business minded, maybe you can relate. When I forget to consult my emotions, I have made grave mistakes. Sometimes I have decided to be so kind that there is no way the other party will have the option of not liking me, which does not work. Other times, I have been rash and made decisions too quickly out of fear, which caused harm to myself and others.

Recently I have taken on a new business partner who is also a psychologist. I find having her in my life I am better able to slow down and check in with my feelings. I choose to turn to her and consult with her on business matters. We make decisions together and I find our decisions are more balanced. When I make a mistake, or see I am not equipped for a task, I go to her, and we decide together on an alternative plan. In the past I often thought I was choosing to be "an independent thinker" or "quick on my feet". Both are defaults. However, I am learning to choose to collaborate. I am learning to choose to build a different type of relationship with my business partner. And these choices have a ripple effect in my positive view of myself and others.

Choosing to notice our feelings allows us to take more meaningful action, which allows us to make more meaning even in the worst of circumstances.

It is hard to like ourselves when we blunder with people. I will tell you, I don't like myself in all of my relationships. Like everyone else, I too struggle to like myself, and there have been many times when I didn't know I was allowed to like myself. I don't remember someone sitting me down as a child saying:

> *"It's okay to have a positive relationship with yourself, even when you make mistakes. It's always good to talk to yourself about what has happened. Oh, and make sure you forgive yourself when you screw up. Make sure you love the parts of you that are mischievous. These parts won't go away, they will cause you embarrassment and hurt, but they are not all bad. So, make sure you remember to make friends with them. You don't need to hide who you truly are. Remember, we are all people like everybody else. Love you no matter what!"*

No fault to any adults that neglected to do this for me, or for you. Most people don't know how to do this for themselves, let alone anyone else.

We can begin to learn to choose to be kind to ourselves, to foster kind thoughts about ourselves, and we can begin to support others to do the same for themselves. We are learning a different thing here. We start saying kind and gracious things to ourselves and to all of the parts of who we are on the inside. And then we can learn to do this for other people. We can get better at offering authentic kindness towards ourselves and others, as often as possible.

When I believe I have a choice about how I am seen by others, I do a better job of choosing to be seen more in my value and less in my defaults. I am not always seen favorably by others. I still make mistakes in relationships. I have flaws! But it is nice to notice all the relationships where I flourish. It is also nice to give myself permission to let go of relationships where I do not like myself.

You are allowed to say goodbye to relationships where other people feel the need to believe the worst about you. You get to say goodbye to relationships where you don't like who you are. You get to move on from relationships where you are hurting others, where you are being hurt, where you don't know how to transform your negative beliefs about yourself or others. This is your choice.

We don't have to stay stuck in the pain of believing we cannot change. It is always unnatural for us to believe we are trapped in an identity where we are pressured to cover up what we have been made to believe is unacceptable. We feel at odds when we live in constant fear of being shamefully exposed and deemed worthy of isolation. We can choose to live as whole people, perfectly-imperfect and whole.

Let me encourage you here. Perhaps no one has ever granted you these permissions, but I am, right now:
You get to feel good about yourself.
You get to see good stuff in you.
You get to trust other people see good stuff in you.
You get to get better at seeing good stuff in others.

Here are some more choices you have, collectively:

You get to have hope for your own humanity and the humanity of others.
You get to have hope for your place in the context of your human relationships.
You get to learn you are valuable enough to be included just as you are.
You get to learn you are not required to be in a relationship with every human you encounter.
You get to honor that someone may be better served apart from you,

Or that you may be better served apart from them.
You get to know it's okay to say goodbye to some relationships and it is okay to hold on to others.

People often say, "I am the common denominator in my relationships." Yes, you are. The same is true for me and my relationships. But you are not the only person in your relationships. We are all flawed and afraid, so we assume us being the common denominator is a negative thing. It is healthy to remember we are in relationships with people who are also flawed and afraid. Every time you experience pain in a relationship, it is not always your fault. It is definitely not always the other person's fault either.

> You hurt people but other people hurt you too. Some hurt isn't processed well in human relationships. This is the common denominator.

This is not a blame game. It is as useless to blame others as it is useless to blame ourselves. Blame doesn't work. Blame feels powerful for a time, but it is a way of avoiding emotion and it draws us away from experiencing that we are loved. I deserve to feel good about who I am in my relationships as much as you deserve to feel good about who you are in your relationships. Other people deserve this as well—whether they know it, or want to believe it, that is their choice.

Contemplative Questions:

Who are you choosing to be in your relationships?

How are your choices serving you?

At this point it is important that we have an explicit conversation about what emotional safety is and what it is not.

Love and Love's Energy

EMOTIONAL SAFETY

"If we are unhappy without a relationship, we'll probably be unhappy with one as well. A relationship doesn't begin our life; a relationship doesn't become our life. A relationship is a continuation of life."
Melody Beattie[1]

When we deny our inner emotional signals, we override our needs and rights for safety in our relationships. Having a better understanding of what is emotional safe is key for you as you go through the content of this book. Moreover, emotional safety is key for your life going forward because understanding what is good emotional safety will help us have better relationships all around. After all, we all have the right to determine what is emotionally safe in all of our relationships.

> Emotional safety is exactly what it sounds like. More than asking ourselves "Am I safe or unsafe with this person?", when we evaluate our emotional safety we build capacity to evaluate if we are safe enough to bring our whole self forward in a relationship and then to trust that the energy we are experiencing is truly loving.

Emotional safety gives us a method to evaluate love. Love gives us a foundation to give and receive emotional safety. Within the balance of love and safety we are better able to listen for the signals of our

---

[1] Beattie, Melody (1990). The Language of Letting Go: Daily Meditations on Codependency. Hazelden Publishing.

emotions and we are better able to express our emotions to ourselves and others. Good emotional safety helps us to cultivate more good emotional safety.

There are some people who are safe to be with, in that they will not sexually or physically abuse us. But they are not safe for us to bring our whole self forward with. Some relationships are healthy enough, but not safe enough for us to risk losing our emotional footing. If we only assess whether relationships are physically and even sexually safe or unsafe, we are not *tuning-in* to our inner world to notice: *Do I feel emotionally safe in this relationship?* Sometimes we call this ability to *tune-in* to our inner world intuition; sometimes we call it insight.

It is okay for us to realize when we do not feel emotionally safe with someone. This does not necessarily make that person a bad person, but we can learn to have emotional distance with some people and emotional closeness with others. We can honor our intuition and lean into our emotional experience, this is a part of the process of discovering emotional safety.

> A mental health professional I deeply respect shared this story with me. An old friend contacted them to go out for dinner and drinks. While they were catching up the friend suggested she had a good opportunity. She suggested that my colleague join her to go to another party where some people would buy them food and alcohol and whatever they wanted. She said that she had made good connections with these men and there was a lot of opportunity to make some side cash. My colleague made an excuse not to go to the party and found a way to wind down the conversation and end the night. To me this is a

great example of intuition and how my colleague was able to use their instinct to avoid what could be harmless fun but sounded more like a very unsafe situation. My colleague was not above the risk of being put at risk, and they intuitively avoided potential danger. They kept themselves emotionally safe.

I am grateful for stories like this one that remind me to stay tuned in to myself. Our intuition can be an asset to keeping us emotionally safe.

Throughout this book stay tuned-in to how you feel as we discuss your relationship with yourself, your relationships with others and your relationship with God. Let the process of developing your emotional safety unfold as it does, knowing that you are permitted to feel uniquely safe or unsafe in your unique relationships. You need not put pressure on yourself to bypass your intuition. No one has the authority to demand you feel emotionally safe in any of your relationships.Take all the time you need to develop your ability to *tune-in* to your own emotions.

Contemplative Questions:

How have you considered emotional safety in the past?

How will you define emotional safety going forward?

Before we move on, I want to remind you of some truths:

You are loved, just the way you are. You are a perfectly-imperfect and a person just like everyone else. There is nothing you need to do to make yourself more valuable. You are loved. You know your inner story of loneliness and fear. You know all your flaws and the ways you cover yourself. This is your reminder, no matter your story, you are still loved.

Trusting we are loved will come and go. A large portion of questioning love is our experience of being loved. We are loveable, we are designed to be loveable, our survival as humans depends on this. Our ability to accept our lovability is rooted in attachment theory. Let's begin to explore the experiences of our lives, and how our attachment story promotes or hinders our *love-energy*.

Tara Boothby

Love and Love's Energy

Tara Boothby

LOVEABLE

Love and Love's Energy

A LIFELONG LOVE STORY

"A securely attached child will store an internal working model of a responsive, loving, reliable caregiver, and of a self that is worthy of love and attention and will bring these assumptions to bear on all other relationships. Conversely, an insecurely attached child may view the world as a dangerous place in which other people are to be treated with great caution and see himself as ineffective and unworthy of love. These assumptions are relatively stable and enduring: those built up in the early years of life are particularly persistent and unlikely to be modified by subsequent experience."
Jeremy Holmes[1]

The above quote is very helpful. With our curiosity piqued about our *internal working model*, we can have compassion for our whole selves.

Attachment is a beautiful stream of psychology deeply rooted in not only our biology but also our evolutionary survival. The next few chapters will bring together some of the main themes of attachment, noticing how this *"love science"* fuels *love-energy*.

---

[1] Holmes, Jeremy (1993). John Bowlby and Attachment Theory :Makers of Modern Psychotherapy. Routledge.

Love and Love's Energy

NATURE, NURTURE, AND THE HEART OF LOVE

"We now know that love is, in actuality, the pinnacle of evolution, the most compelling survival mechanism of the human species. Not because it induces us to mate and reproduce. We do manage to mate without love! But because love drives us to bond emotionally with a precious few others who offer us safe haven from the storms of life. Love is our bulwark, designed to provide emotional protection and we cope with the ups and downs of existence. This drive to emotionally attach — to find someone to whom we can turn and say "Hold me tight" — is wired into our genes and our bodies. It is as basic to life, health, and happiness as the drives for food, shelter, or sex. We need emotional attachments with a few irreplaceable others to be physically and mentally healthy — to survive."
Sue Johnson[1]

We are social, emotional, intellectual, physical, occupational and spiritual beings.[2] These dimensions, all of this design, offer structure to prove how we have been knit together with a need not only to survive and excel in the nature of our being, but also, to thrive in our lives by the vital discovery of nurture for our relationships.

---

[1] Johnson, Sue (2008). Hold Me Tight: Seven Conversations for a Lifetime of Love. Little, Brown Spark.

[2] Boothby, Tara (2005). The Young Love Project. Thesis Research Trinity Wester University.

The scientific nature of who we are is not enough on its own. Relationships are a necessary contributor to our evolutionary survival. We need people, people are meant to nurture each other. Infants die without a caregiver.[1] Being cared for is not a superficial need. Without nurturing life really does end, even though the risk of death from lack of relationship lessens as we age. We will likely stay alive with limited or even adequate relationships, but the less nurture we experience, parts of us, psychologically, neurologically and biologically, continue to die.

> We are hardwired for love. Love is not a superficial need. It cannot be neglected. Even evolutionary psychology confirms this: our nature needs to be nurtured for our survival.

Without the loving presence of a caregiver, parts of our brain shut down, the development of neural pathways in our brains is limited, our physical health will deteriorate, we might have bad gut health or physical somatic symptoms, there are many, many correlated risks.[2] So, what is this nurture? We may say that nurturing care is the overarching term for attachment theory and *love-energy*.[3]

Not only is our biology dependent on nurture but also our psychological wellbeing. What are the psychological implications for us when our experience of nurturing is limited? Our thoughts and beliefs about who we are, who people are, what the world is like can be impacted for the worse. We are more likely to see

---

[1] DeBellis, Michael D; Woolley, Donald P., Hooper, Stephen R. (2013). Neuropsychological Findings in Pediatric Maltreatment: Relationship of PTSD, Dissociative Symptoms, and Abuse/Neglect Indices to Neurocognitive Outcomes. Child Maltreatment 18(3), 171-183.

[2] Seigel, Daniel J. (2020). The Developing Mind: How Relationships and the Brain Interact to Shape Who We Are. The Guilford Press.

[3] Bowlby, John. (1969). Attachment and Loss: Volume One. Basic Books.

things as negative.[1] With a negative view comes negative automatic thoughts.[2] These perceptions are based on our version of *"I belong alone,"* reinforced by the parts of ourselves we are desperate to cover up (our unique formula of covering our flaws with defaults). Our human nature kicks into survival mode to protect us. Our crafty minds strategize for survival.

Believing negative thoughts about ourselves, other people and the world will cause us to hide our flawed nature. Hiding, or defaulting, becomes a means of survival (I think it is possible to even notice this as an evolutionary adaptation). Hiding our flaws is a way to try to maintain some semblance of nurture. We are afraid others will see our flaws and reject us.[3]

Nurture truly does benefit relationships, however neglect also has lasting impact. Experiences of neglect in our relationships increase our automatic negative beliefs. Without intervention, we may not have an opportunity to change our faulty thinking. Some will have mental health problems for the rest of our lives. Some will have severe pathology, and some will have mild quirks.[4]

We share a common human experience, yet we all have our own unique version of this experience. Our unique positive ways of looking at things and our unique negative ways of looking at things.

Our childhood experiences of love inspire us, for the better or the worse. It informs our ability to offer love as adults, and the methods we develop to live in relationships with others. It is hard to stabilize our

---

[1] Amen, Daniel (2023). Conquer Your Negative Thoughts: The secret to Emotional Freedom and Happiness. Tyndale Refresh.

[3] Johnson, Sue (2013). Love Sense: The Revolutionary New Science of Romantic Relationships. Little, Brown Spark.

[4] Amen, Daniel (2023). Conquer Your Negative Thoughts: The secret to Emotional Freedom and Happiness. Tyndale Refresh.

feelings when we are living in survival mode. When a child has limited experience of nurturing love from a caregiver, limited modeling of emotional regulation, limited coregulation, this child determines for themselves how to be in the world around them as an adult. In moments when our need for nurture goes unmet, we may explode our emotions, or we may implode our emotions.

> What it might look like for people to explode their feelings or implode their feelings is really quite fascinating. Let's say two people have a similar negative belief, "People don't really like me." One person chooses to explode their feelings and act out. They may be *verbally aggressive, or violent, they may commit crime, or become promiscuous, or they may simply be vocal or vibrant, or always up for a good debate*. The other person who has the same belief of, "People don't really like me." may implode their feelings about this belief. This person may *withdraw from relationships, they may self-harm, or they may derogate relationships and judge things that are safe as unsafe, all to avoid* their fear of not measuring up to the belief "People don't really like me.".

> Let's consider one more example. Suppose two people share another very tricky negative belief, "Everyone has to like me." One person may explode their feelings about this in seemingly positive ways. This person may be *driven to be extra charming, over the top with gift giving, extravagant at throwing parties, spending lots of money and bragging loudly about it*. The other person may implode their feelings about this

> belief, "Everyone has to like me" in other seemingly positive ways. They may *find opportunities to quietly pay attention and notice subtleties about people and then surprise them with perfect gift giving, they may work diligently at their job and go above and beyond on every task all behind the scene, hoping for praise, or they may simply be someone who seeks out one-on-one interactions and in these interactions deeply listens and deeply connects to sooth their own longing to be liked.*

Both of these examples illustrate how our automatic negative thoughts influence our strategies, the way we default in the world around us, how we explode or implode our feelings. Remember the word "automatic" is very important here, when we live on *autopilot* whether our response to a situation is good or bad, it is automatic, and we are not presenting our true whole self in our response, we are defaulting.

> Having received limited love in our formative relationships, then having a limited ability to practice self-love, we develop our emotional regulation based on what has worked and what has not worked for us our entire story.

> Our need to survive influences our relationships as much as our relationships influence our quality of surviving. When we experience loving human relationships, positive things happen. For example, we have hope and take courage from these relationships. We are better able to venture to believe in love, in general. We are hard-wired for love, and love is beautiful to wonder on.

As we participate in *love-energy* our minds are renewed. Not only do we enjoy believing in love, but our bodies respond and function better. We thrive by nurture.

My hope is you will let your curiosity about loving people nudge you at your own pace. As you love other people, and yourself, just be curious. One day, you will wake up and you will look in the mirror, straight in your own eyes and say: *"I'm kinda good at this love thing. I no longer feel the need to hide any part of who I am! What's so bad about me? For that matter, what is so bad about anyone else?"*

We are designed with such beautiful complexity. Every human life is complex, hard to hold at times, yet worthy of being held for no other reason than each one of us exists.

We are complex, messy beings, living lives full of trial and error, full of highs and lows, in and out of relationships, feeling the peace and potency of getting it right for one another, feeling the pain and panic of getting it wrong. Always in this continuous dilemma of our love discovery.

We are all just people like everybody else, sometimes we get things right and sometimes we get things wrong; we are people, and we will make mistakes at times. Even great people, people better than you or me, get some of it wrong. You and I have many relationships we juggle, all of which are filled with good and bad. We are messy people, each of us—all of us with our own story. My mess limits me at times and your mess will limit you at times. And yet, we are always loved, loveable and loving. Always learning....

"The message is in the mess."
Kent Hoffman[1]

---

[1] Hoffman, Kent (2015). eightysevenminutes.com.

Contemplative Question (remember, these questions are here for you to interact with as you see fit, they are to further encourage you and pique your curiosity).:

What has your unique experience of nurture taught you about your unique nature?

What feelings are safe to be seen and what feelings are not?

Do you implode or explode your feelings? How do you see yourself doing this?

What are some of your automatic negative thoughts?

It is encouraging to be reminded that our attachment longings are hardwired into our biological make up. Attachment is for our survival.

Love and Love's Energy

NURTURING ATTACHMENTS

"Unconditional parental love is the indispensable nutrient for the child's healthy emotional growth. The first task is to create space in the child's heart for the certainty that she is precisely the person the parents want and love. She does not have to do anything or be any different to earn that love - in fact, she cannot do anything, since that love cannot be won or lost.... The child can be ornery, unpleasant, whiny, uncooperative, and plain rude, and the parent still lets her feel loved. Ways have to be found to convey the unacceptability of certain behaviors without making the child herself feel unaccepted. She has to be able to bring her unrest, her least likable characteristics to the parent and still receive the parent's absolutely satisfying, security-inducing unconditional love."
Gordon Neufeld & Gabor Mate[1]

Let's revisit the concept of "our side of the street." Keep in mind that the thing about our side of the street is that we don't get to choose our real-estate. Our real-estate was bought and paid for by our parents. How we have learned to care for our side of the street is deeply rooted in our relationship with those who determined where our life would be planted — our birth parents and/or our primary caregivers; holding space that we live in a world of unique family stories, therefore we are allowed to have our own unique definition of who cared for us in our early years, as well our own pain around who should have cared for us but did not.

---

[1] Neufeld, Gordon, Mate, Gabor (2006). Hold On To Your Kids: Why Parents Need To Matter More Than Peers. Ballentine Books.

> Signing up to be a primary symbol of attachment is one of the most influential decisions someone will make for another person's life.

If you were raised with a primary attachment figure and a secondary attachment figure, two grownups who agree to be vital to your beginning, then you are truly blessed. Some are blessed even further to have other adults like aunts and uncles, grandparents, etc. Other caregivers present and providing care for them during childhood. Some of us have the genuine benefit of being planted firmly in a community of love. Others of us are haunted by the ache of having limited attachment experiences, or inconsistent unpredictable care, or worse.

The research highlights that the more positive experiences young children have with their caregivers the better equipped these children are as they grow to be adults who create positive patterns in their future family life and relationships.[1] The more *love-energy* the attachment figure offers, the better the child will understand what love is and is not. The more attachment figures present in a child's life, the more the child will understand there is a variety of love. This child will likely have a deeper sense of what is emotional safety and what is not.

The fewer positive interactions with their primary caregiver, the harder it is for children to believe any relationship will be good. The fewer experiences of other positive adults who offer loving interactions to a child, the harder it is for such a child to believe relationships will be good. Children need adults who are kind, adults who communicate belief in this unique child's value. Positive interactions with adults benefit

---

[1] Daines, Chantel L., Hansen, Dustin, Lelinneth B. Novilla, M., Crandall, AliceAnn (2021). Effects of a Positive and Negative Childhood Experience on Adult Family Health. BMC Health, Article number: 651.

all children to promote their emotional, psychological, and developmental growth.[1]

Suppose a child grows up with two parents and along with siblings has an extended family living close by of aunts and uncles, cousins and grandparents. This child is in a good school with many friends. On hot summer days this child goes to their grandmother's house and runs through her sprinklers, plays with other neighborhood children, and does crafts and baking with their grandma. Their grandmother is tender and loving and joyful toward them. She is friendly and fair, and also challenges them on mischievous behavior. When the child comes home after a fun day with grandma their father welcomes them to hear and delight in all the stories of their day. The family has bedtime routines, and eats meals together, they watch movies, and go for walks as a unit. They play together, they celebrate the good times, and they come together to address the bad times. This family is not perfect, but they have space for mistakes because they have taken the time to build relationships with each other.

What might the future look like for this child? We can expect that this child will continue to have supportive relationships like these and move forward into their adult life with better opportunity and great ability to benefit from the opportunities they are afforded.

Suppose another child is born to a single mother. She left her home at a young age and shortly after found out she was pregnant, which was a great

[1] Neufeld, Gordon, Mate, Gabor (2006). Hold On To Your Kids: Why Parents Need To Matter More Than Peers. Ballentine Books.

surprise. She had little money, no education, and a low paying job. She is on her own caring for this child. This mother does not know what to do so she asks for help wherever she can find it. She researches every community support she can find. She signs up for community parent classes, she finds a federal education program for single mothers, she finds other single mothers who have similar goals, and they create a community around their children. This child will experience that their mother is working diligently to provide for their family. At times this mother is exhausted and overwhelmed and will not be able to offer as much support as a coparenting home, but as this child ages, they will have more and more insight, which will help them to make sense of some of the hard choices their mother had to make. And because this mother is so loving and sacrificing, as this child ages they and their mother talk about the hard times growing up, because this child is so very loved.

What might the future look like for this child? They will likely have to work harder than some other young adults, but this child has many experiences of love and support from their mom and has seen their mom model resilience. It is likely this child has inherited a resilient attitude and will apply fortitude as they saw in the example of their mother. They may be afforded fewer opportunities, but they will likely have the ingenuity to find opportunities, as they have observed in their mother's example.

But some stories are so very sad. Suppose a child is born into a very dangerous home situation. As a toddler this child is taken from their birth parents, and their grandparents do not know how to work with the child welfare system so this child is put into federal care. The child is placed into one foster home, then another, then another, then another. Finally, the child lands in a group home. The young adults who provide care for this child and the other preteens and teens are friendly and caring, they are kind. They provide food and tell all the group home kids when to go to bed, when to shower, to knock it off when they start conflict, and they are happy for all the kids when they do well in school. Then one day this child turns 18. This child has had instrumental love, love that meets basic needs for survival,[1] but they have missed out on the love that other children have provided, love that goes beyond providing for basic human needs for survival.

What might the future look like for this child? It is very hard to predict a future for a child who experiences such neglect. Unfortunately, the day this child leaves the system of care they are likely the only one fighting for their future. Their future is unpredictable, and the harder the circumstances they face in their young adult life the less likely they will reach the same potential as the other two children.

Attachment theory alone is not enough. Adults need to intentionally nurture the children in their care to promote positive *love-energy* moments with their kids, so these kids have hope for love to be nurtured in their future. The more love a child is given the higher capacity they will have to do the same nurturing in all

---

[1] Main, Mary (2003). *Adult Attachment Scoring and Classification Systems (Version 7.2)*. Department of Psychology, University of California, Berkeley.

of their future relationships; to grow to be adults who will be better able to give and receive *love-energy*.

When a child has an adult in their life that knows them as both good and not-so-good, and loves them the way they are, this child learns to see themselves as good and not-so-good, and learns they are loved just the way they are. This child has already begun to understand their whole self is included. This child has already begun to understand they are loved, loveable and loving.

Loving our unlovable parts is always a work in progress. Loving others' unlovable parts takes just as much practice. When people around us love and accept us, we are better able to accept our own unlovable parts. And parents are key to helping children discover the inclusivity of love.

There is no such thing as perfect parenting. The circle of security (COS) orgininators say, *"the goal is good enough parenting."*[1] Parenting strategies are helpful, but doing the right things for your kids will not benefit them if you do not slow down and learn how to manifest love.

When we have more loving experiences in our childhood, we are more likely to become adults who accept ourselves, our whole selves.

> Parenting is not a performance. Love builds a child up, so they are able to say: *"My parent hears me with loving ears, sees me with loving eyes, and knows me with a loving mind, as often as possible."* This is a great relationship for them to launch from into the world around them. This is a great

[1] Hoffman, Kent, Copper, Glen, Powell, Bert (2017). *Raising a Secure Child How Circle of Security Parenting Can Help You Nurture Your Child's Attachment, Emotional Resilience, and Freedom to Explore.* Guilford Press.

relationship for them to return to when the world has left them tired and lonely.

Parenting is not about collecting the right moves and using these moves at the right times. Parenting is messy. It is hard work riddled with mistakes. Parenting is emotional, and emotionally draining. It is consistently inconsistent. Parenting requires us to be mindful of how we are informed by our own trauma and attachment wounds so we can pivot as needed. Love is the goal for parenting. The goal is for us to slow down to notice our loving parenting efforts because when we do we increase our ability to also catch our parenting blunders. We see the good and we see the bad, and our observing of ourselves helps us refine our *good enough parenting*.

> Allow yourself to feel good about the moments you get it right as a parent. Allow yourself to savor when you do *love-energy* parenting. Kids learn *love-energy* from their caregivers. Kids are not worried about having perfect parents. Like everybody else, children feel loved in moments of corrective epiphany — small moments where a child feels loved for no other reason than the reason they exist.

Relaxing into the belief *love-energy* is the answer for our relationships with people is not easy. It sounds good, but we know it is not easy. I know this because there are days when I get it wrong for my kids, my husband, myself, my colleagues, and even at times for clients. There will be days when you get it wrong too. But when we are mindful of what is loving, we are more likely to practice being loving to others, and to catch our mistakes and love ourselves in these moments. Then we decide how and when we repair with others, and with our own self.

Take a few moments to think about what you believe about *love-energy*.

Contemplative Questions:

How have you experienced love over the years, the good and the bad?

What messages were you raised to believe about yourself and others?

What messages were you taught about love? How has this impacted you?

Who were your key attachment figures and how well did they express to you that you are loved, loveable, and loving?

Parenting is strongly associated with attachment. We have touched on this here and in the next couple chapters we will focus primarily on parents and parenting. Don't skip it! It is all relevant. Even those of us who are not parents will better understand ourselves by understanding the relational position of parents. After all, we are all somebody's child.

> Parenting is the core contributor for attachment, and attachment is core to *love-energy*.

PARENT GUILT

"What cannot be communicated to the mother cannot be communicated to the self."
John Bowlby[1]

Guilt and parenting really do seem synonymous. Even great parents are perfectly-imperfect parents. We are all just people like everybody else, parents are just people too; people in charge of little lives, people with one of the most sacred responsibilities in the whole world. And it can feel so shameful when we make mistakes with our kids, which we do, daily. Parenting is trial and error. The erroring gets us parents feeling guilty and then we often find ourselves comparing ourselves to what we imagine is the mass success other parents are achieving. This is a very normal struggle to get stuck in, but it is detrimental to get stuck in feeling guilty about our parenting flaws, there are little lives depending on us.

Why do we feel guilty as parents? We have a lot we are contending with:

> *We get frustrated. We have to be disciplinarians. We cave and give in. We hover. We criticize. We meddle. We compare. We overcommit our children. We shame them. We coerce affection from them. We overprotect. We attempt to toughen them up.*

The Bowlby quote (in the epigraph above) makes sense on a deep emotional level. When children have

---

[1] Interview, unknown reference

a felt awareness of not being able to communicate something with our own primary caregiver, then we will struggle to identify, regulate, integrate, to communicate what we do not trust is acceptable. Our parents teach us what is acceptable and unacceptable.

> Children bring their whole way of being to their caregiver to find out what will be received and what will not like: *shame, fear, sadness, joy, curiosity, anger, pain, hunger, humor, achievements, lust, anxiety, sullenness, disgust, depression, questions, conflict with peers, conflict with siblings, getting loud, being mischievous, being helpful, mimicking behaviors, exploring their little worlds, expanding their sense of self, every part of their little life — things that cause their little minds concern and things they want to know are to be enjoyed.*

Children communicate their thoughts and feelings to their parents from a very early age. These emotions and concepts will be constructed as good or bad. While children are very young, we frequently notice the earliest emotions as *anger, surprise, disgust, enjoyment, fear, and sadness.*[1] The study of neurology also confirms the early life affect experiences of *seeking, rage, lust, care, grief/panic, and play.*[2] From a very, very young age children are developing their experience of emotions and then their constructs of emotion, and a child's experience with their caregiver leads them to determine what is flawed about them, and how they should avoid or cover up their flaws.

There are no definitive answers about how a child will adapt when their core emotions are mishandled. But it

---

[1] Ekman, Paul, Friesen, Wallace V. (1975). *Unmasking The Face: A Guide to Recognizing Emotions From Facial Expressions.* Prentice-Hall.

[2] Paulsen, Sandra (2017). *When There Are No Words: Repairing Early Trauma and Neglect From the Attachment Period With EMDR Therapy.* CreateSpace Independent Publishing Platform.

is worth wondering about. Have you taken time to wonder about how your early emotions were accepted or rejected by your caregivers? Here are a few scenarios to contemplate. Feel free to even come up with your own answers:

> When a child is frightened by a bad dream and calls for their parent, and no one comes, what constructs might this child develop about their own fear? What might they construct about vulnerability?
>
> When a child is angry and their parent gets angrier, what constructs might a child develop about their own anger, and what might the construct about other people's anger?
>
> When a child is proud of themselves and shows their caregiver proof of their accomplishment and they are teased, what constructs might this child develop about their achievements? About their curiosity? About delighting in themselves? What might they learn about seeking praise or approval?
>
> Or a child who is happy, happy, happy and singing their little song, then hears their big person say, "Can you shut up? I am trying to think!" What might this child construct about being happy? What beliefs might this child form about other people?

Most babies can sense into their relationship with their primary caregiver and notice what is well received and what is rejected. Then the baby adapts. As this baby has more success with what is accepted by their caregiver, they continue to do the acceptable things and hide away the unacceptable.[1] Then the infant continues to create their pattern of hiding or showing their needs based on what has gotten them attention from their caregiver. By the time this child enters school, they already have most of their cognitive constructs, their automatic thoughts, and behavioral defaults in place. We commonly refer to this as *attachment styles*.[2] Some parents respond with over-the-top emotional expression, while others are more muted in their responses. Some have their goals and objectives for their own role in parenting as well as their goals and objectives for their kids. All parents have their own flaws they are covering; they have their own constructs and their own defaults which influence how they parent. Each parent has their own unique twist on how they parent based on their system of defaults. The parents' unique twist is compounded by how each unique child makes their own interpretations of how what they do is accepted or rejected by their caregiver. This is fascinating.

> Parent-child relationships are always completely unique adventures. Caregiving is always a *"choose your own adventure"* story.

No matter the child, no matter the unique difficulties or dilemmas unique to each unique child, we need also to remember that no matter the child, the success of the relationship rises and falls on the parent's position.

> Parents parent, not children.

There is some predictability of how the parent's way of being will impact the child's pattern of defaults, but there are no definitive formulas. Each parent-child relationship is unique. Each child will have their

---

[1] Bowlby, John. (2012). *The Making and Breaking of Affectional Bonds (Routledge Classics)*. Routledge.

[2] Clinton, Tim, Sibcy, Gary (2009). *Attachments: Why You Love, Feel, and Act the Way You Do*. Thomas Nelson.

unique struggle with feeling flawed in their relationship with their parent. Each child will start to wonder about how lonely they feel. Each child will start to practice and fine tune their default way of being. Each child is unique. This makes parenting beautiful and extremely tricky. Even great parents still have some ruptures in their relationship with their kids.[1]

All people are building up their strategies to survive their lives, even children. And parents are observing their children and trying to guide their child's behaviors. Parents want their children to behave in a way that is pleasing. Pleasing to what? I am not 100% sure, I honestly think we make up our parenting expectations based on who we are and how we have strategized and defaulted in our lives. But based on a parent's approval or disapproval children will adapt to hide or express what each individual child sees pleases their parents.[2]

> Here are some needs one child may hide and another child may amplify: *one-on-one attention, solitude, good behaviors, bad behaviors, being in line with family rules, keeping family traditions, breaking rules, rebellion, showing off, expressing their point of view, asking for help, seeking comfort, disclosing mistakes, asking for repair, offering repair, taking risks, trying new things, independence, having fun, being playful, sharing successes, being creative, expressing sadness, expressing anger, participating*

---

[1] Hoffman, Kent, Copper, Glen, Powell, Bert (2017). *Raising a Secure Child How Circle of Security Parenting Can Help You Nurture Your Child's Attachment, Emotional Resilience, and Freedom to Explore.* Guilford Press.

[2] Hoffman, Kent, Copper, Glen, Powell, Bert (2017). Raising a Secure Child How Circle of Security Parenting Can Help You Nurture Your Child's Attachment, Emotional Resilience, and Freedom to Explore. Guilford Press.

> *in conversation, listening, seeing the good in people, being cautious, taking risks, and so on.*

There is no perfect parenting plan, but hopefully we catch some of the moments where our children are seeking to be known. Hopefully we notice how they hide or heighten their need for connection with us. Hopefully our children have more experiences of being accepted than not. Hopefully we manage our guilt and make meaning from it.

The important thing is that we offer our children experiences where they are assured they can come to us and access our support. Parental acceptance does help children feel less flawed in their inevitable mistakes. Parental accessibility does help children carry a less potent version of *"I belong alone."* Parental acceptance and accessibility gives children a better template to construct how to be in their world in more authentic ways.[1] These children will develop more capacity to bring forth their whole selves more often.

Parents are sometimes cast as the easy scapegoat in attachment theory, but they are not. Parents are the most important influence to help children fall in love with love.

> A simple parenting meditation might be to reflect on how to offer love to your children in abundance, at their pace, with their consent, while being informed by your child's unique way of being.

Even slowing down enough to sit in the presence of these words is a valuable parenting practice.

---

[1] Furrow, James L., Palmer, Gail, Johnson, Sue M., Faller, George, Palmer-Olsen, Lisa (2019). Emotionally Focused Family Therapy: Restoring Connection and Promoting Resilience. Routledge.

When parental guilt kicks in, be curious. Listen and discover. Parenting is a work in progress. Self-compassion and gentleness are paramount to love-based parenting.

In family therapy, I like to highlight with parents the value of their presence, particularly when a child expresses some hurt or fear about their lack of value and a parent is witness to their child's vulnerable need. Simple moment. When parents slow down and take time to be simply present these moments carry huge impact. Here is a list of many examples of these big, little, simple, not-simple moments. There are countless opportunities this list is just the beginning:

Sitting with your child, knocking on their door to check in and say hi for no reason, making their favorite food for dinner, eating together, laughing together, driving them to their friends or sports, making jokes, playing with them, praying with them, talking with them, listening to them, laughing at their jokes, being kind, complimenting, celebrating their lives, hugs, kisses, banter, being playful, playing games, laughing, dancing, being spontaneous, tucking them in, smiling at them, apologizing, helping them succeed, getting to know their interests. Being present.

Listening on its own is a powerful parenting skill. Slowing down in order to listen to our children has an enormous impact on them. We start with listening and let the seeing and knowing parts of parental love naturally follow.

> When parents get this — hearing with loving ears, seeing with loving eyes, knowing with a loving mind — I like to wonder with parents: *"Imagine if you had someone to come alongside of you like this?"*

> Listening well soothes our children's attachment fear and yearnings.[1]

When we believe we are required to be perfect in our parenting, it is always easy to lose our emotional footing. When we lose our footing as parents, we often become emotionally unsafe for our children. We expect there is a right way to do the parent role. But in the big moments, good parenting is almost always about keeping things simple:

> *Simply listening.*
>
> *Simply maintaining our self-regulation so our children can co-regulate with us.*
>
> *Making time to be present with our children in the day-to-day of their simple lives.*
>
> *This is the foundation for a lifetime of love between us and our kids.*

When our child gets something wrong for themselves, for the people in their little world, or for us, we practice being present. In a moment, we hear them, we see them, we know them. Our job is to maintain our inner balance and to not worry about the perfect words or deeds of our parenting.

We have permission to offer simple responses in these times. A few words strung together in no grammatical brilliance, or a subtle gesture. A simple response can make a great difference in a child's life:

> *"I forgive you"; "I hear you"; "I see you"; "I love you just the way you are"; "I love you." Or, a gesture: a hug, a nod, a pat on the knee, a fist bump, a squeeze of their shoulder, a wink, a big sigh, eye contact, cuddles, going for a walk, going in and sitting on*

---

[1] Johnson, Sue (2019). *Attachment Theory in Practice: Emotionally Focused Therapy (EFT) with Individuals, Couples, and Families.* The Guilford Press.

their bed, coffee dates, burger dates, making time to talk things through, being consistent, taking serious things seriously, gentle correction, and repair— always repair.

People will say some version of: *"Be the person you never had when you were young."*

How do we learn to be better listeners? It starts with listening. Learning to hear, then see, then know our little ones. You want to be a better parent? Get still and listen in the big moments and in the small ones. You want to be a better person, spouse, colleague, or friend? Do the same. As a child makes attempts at communicating, as they attempt to be heard, and they have experiences where they see their message is accepted by their primary caregivers, they are better able to integrate these moments into their sense of self, to construct greater hope for acceptance and less fear of rejection. These children have an increased capacity to receive and give love-energy.

When you sign up to be a parent, you sign up to help babies grow into children who grow into adults. You create, or come alongside, a life in the fullness of its budding biological, psychological, social, emotional, and spiritual being. This is exactly why caregiving is overwhelming.

There is a lot of life to keep alive in children, and it is all up to you. Can I encourage you to stop aiming for an A+ on this project. This is a living, breathing, always changing relationship, between two whole people who are both developing and changing always.

> The A+ of parenting is a moving target. We will always fail when we only focus on the rules of parenting because the *how-to* book keeps changing.

Contemplative Questions:

Are you a parent? What is your child learning they can and cannot communicate to you?

You are somebody's child. What did you learn you could and could not communicate to your parents?

And how does this continue to impact you and your current relationships?

Talking about parenting definitely stirs up guilt and other uncomfortable emotions. The next chapter is on parental value so don't lose hope, you belong.

PARENTAL VALUE

"You can say the right thing, but if your heart isn't in it, it won't draw you any closer to your child. In fact, fudging may cause you to lose credibility with your child, which can drive a wedge in your relationship. Be sure, therefore, that you truly understand your child before you say you do. If you're not sure whether you understand, simply reflect back what you see and hear."
John M. Gottman[1]

Although this chapter is titled *"Parental Value"* it is important to acknowledge that many individuals who parent children are not biological parents or may never have the title of parent. If you have had neglectful or absent parents it may be helpful to consider another adult in your childhood who provided you with care. Or it may feel safer to consider your experience of being a caregiver, or how as an adult you observe others providing care and parenting to the children in your life.

> Curiosity is one of the most under-rated parenting skills.

When parents and caregivers slow down to make sense of our children's world with them, we are valuing our role as caregiver and their role as child, in this space the energy of love flows. There is a great deal of life our children are living, and a great deal to be curious

---

[1] Gottman, John (1997). *Raising An Emotionally Intelligent Child.* Simon & Schuster.

about. Let's keep in mind how much primary caregivers, parents, are mindful of:

> *Keep them alive, keep them healthy, comfort them when they are sick or hurt, feed them, clothe them, teach them to take care of themselves at their developmental pace, learn about development, make space for their big feelings, hear their emotions, hang in there as they start to not like you, give them space to protest, give them space to be individuals, give them space to be funny, give them space to learn, let them find friends for themselves, help them navigate their friendships, let them go off on their own, watch their independence grow, keep getting to know their personality as it continues to develop and be expressed, get mad at them, repair with them, fail them, repair with them, correct them, hurt their feelings, hurt more feelings, repair with them, support their highs and lows of friendships, their dating life, their mistakes, their struggles with school, their spiritual formation, their academic pursuits, and so on.*

There is much to learn. A great deal for us as caregivers to help our children communicate. Many things for us to be present for. Many, many things for us to be curious about. The pressure is always on.

Primary caregivers are not to blame for all of our inner fear and flaws, but those of us who care for children do have a part to play in the beliefs our children form about relationships and love. The long list above normalizes how many things we aim to get right for our kids. This list also normalizes how likely it is we will err on some points.

What is pivotal to our caregiving is our hope for our children's budding self, as well as our hope for our presence in their life. Our parental value, our value as caregivers, is to learn to notice our positive intention toward our children and to harness this intention as often as possible.[1]

All caregivers are learning to trust our parenting ability, to have good intention, to be reasonable about our limits, and to be aware of our abundant love for our children. This is a constant work in progress.

We don't have to get it perfect for our kids. In fact, we won't always get it perfect for our kids. But let's put emphasis on the right things here: Parental care is about listening—providing opportunities for our children to have many experiences of being heard and accepted by us, when they show up with whatever they need to show up with.[2]

Parenting is caregiving, and it is about holding space for the good, the bad, and the ugly.

There will be times of:

> *"I hate you" and "You're a bad mommy." Physical injuries you cannot prevent. Broken bones you are sure you could have prevented. Times you feel betrayed by your co-parent. Times you and your partner have friction and disagreement. Times you feel left out and left behind. Anger, sorrow, rage, fear, tantrums, slammed doors, ignored texts and calls, friends you disapprove of, mismanaged money, hobbies and interests you do not understand. There will be music (some good and some bad). There*

---

[1] Hoffman, Kent, Copper, Glen, Powell, Bert (2017). *Raising a Secure Child How Circle of Security Parenting Can Help You Nurture Your Child's Attachment, Emotional Resilience, and Freedom to Explore.* Guilford Press.

[2] Furrow, James L., Palmer, Gail, Johnson, Sue M., Faller, George, Palmer-Olsen, Lisa (2019). *Emotionally Focused Family Therapy: Restoring Connection and Promoting Resilience.* Routledge.

will be all the things. All the bad and the ugly, but all the beautiful as well. And you will get some things wrong and some things right.

Our children, just like everyone else, are wired to long for us to say: *"I hear you."* All the things our children say and do that don't make sense to us, all the things they say and do that do make sense to us, all are valuable. Remember: we start with listening to our children, and the seeing them for who they are in all their unique brilliance, and then knowing them in their stunning individuality will follow.

Whether we are biological parents, or caregivers we are in charge of a little life. A life we are helping to sculpt. As this little person is supported to fumble around in their relationship with us and still be found by us, we make space for their confusion and their emotion. When we get it right for them (or eventually get it right for them), they have surer footing about their ability to be authentic and whole in the world.

Remember, nurture is a part of our evolutionary survival.[1] At every age, we continue to long for nurture, especially from our caregivers. You and I both know this. We were once kids. We are always somebody's kid. We are all people, and we all have families. No matter the course of our family relationships our desire to share our authentic self with our core relationships, with the people we have had the longest relationships with, is always potent. How many people go their whole lives wondering if they have ever been truly known by the people that should matter the most to them?

If you are someone who is out of relationship with your parents or primary caregivers, this can be very painful. If you have had to draw boundaries with your

---

[1] Bowlby, John. (1988). *A Secure Base: Parent-Child Attachment and Healthy Human Development.* Basic Books.

caregivers because they were unsafe, drawing boundaries like this takes a great deal of courage and strength. If your caregivers took off, or gave you up, this is a major void, and it is okay if it feels like nothing will ever fill it. If your parents have passed away and you are orphaned, it is okay to notice how this hollow grief complicates your longing. Wounds in our own relationships with the people who were supposed to care for us are all some level of trauma. Be gentle with your inner child hurts.

Remember, you are the person who is taking the time to read this book and think these thoughts about love. Listen to yourself with loving ears, see yourself with loving eyes, and know yourself with a loving mind. All of the parts of yourself belong, the young and the old, the flawed and the fabulous.

> Attachment is the theory behind our experience and expression of *love-energy*. We are born into the world with a natural tendency toward love. Love is hardwired into our survival strategy.[1] When our need for nurturing has not been met, we carry this loss with us, this loss impacts our personhood and all of our relationships.

---

[1] Bowlby, John. (1988). *A Secure Base: Parent-Child Attachment and Healthy Human Development.* Basic Books.

Contemplative questions:

Did you have relationship with your biological parents as a child? How did your parents presence or absence impact you?

What does the term caregiver mean to you? Which adults in your story provided you with caregiving?

How did your parents do at listening to you? How about your caregivers?

How did your parents do at valuing you? How about your caregivers?

If you are a parent, how well are you doing at listening to your kids?

How well are you doing at valuing your kids?

We are well into our discussion on attachment theory and how parents are key to how their children are able to move freely in and out of relationships. The stories of how children have been neglected and abused are always painful to learn. Let's continue to offer space to further explore how it is that some parents forget the miracle of the small life they are caring for.

FORGOTTEN MIRACLES

"Young children, who for whatever reason are deprived of the continuous care and attention of a mother or a substitute-mother, are not only temporarily disturbed by such deprivation, but may in some cases suffer long-term effects which persist."
John Bowlby

I loved being pregnant with both of my children, but there was something absolutely magical about being pregnant with my first child. I loved feeling like a fat lazy kitten. I loved eating candy and fresh pineapple. I also loved every minute of being in the hospital when it was finally time for her arrival. All of it was magic to me. I was beyond excited to meet our daughter, so much so, that I did not make time to worry about what was coming after our meeting. I had not paused to consider I had no idea how to be a parent. Even though I was an attachment focused therapist, when our daughter arrived, I still had no clue how this momma was going to care for this baby.

All of the months of being pregnant led me to an amazing transformative moment when our baby girl was born. A moment in which I was forever changed. I was a mother. I had done something phenomenal. I had participated in creating something, and not just any something, I participated in creating a life!

For me becoming a mother was the most magical magic. Then, that first night she went to sleep. And I couldn't believe it. A miracle was asleep in our house! How could I ever return to normal life? I sat on my La-Z-Boy and obsessed over this question: "Will I ever relax again? Do people watch Netflix after they have performed a miracle?" And I cried.

But I did return to Netflix, and social media, and driving by myself leaving my baby miles away from me. I went back to work. The routine of daily living adjusted itself. The potency of my miracle lost its vibrance. I was a mother and I was still a person.

We live in a world that keeps spinning, and we are good at hopping back on the rotation. We have done it our whole lives. We hop back on the rotation and, on some level, we get off track from our child.

When the miracle part of having a baby gets forgotten, we start missing out on *love-energy* with our little baby. Then the baby grows and ages and we keep missing *love-energy* moments. Because our little person is hardwired to want to be in relationship with us, their little minds cannot fathom why we would miss their needs, miss their moments, neglect to see their attempts to be noticed. After a while they try to figure out what is wrong with them and *why we leave them alone*. They start writing their own story of *"I belong alone."*

The more exaggerated the parenting errors, the more exaggerated the child's story of *"I belong alone."* We know this is true because we are all somebody's child. It is not helpful to blame our parents, but noticing the ways we were hurt as children helps our recovery. It also helps us to be honest about how we positively and negatively impact our children's view of themselves.

Children are impacted by how they are supported to understand their life. Children are impacted by the caring they receive and the caring they go without. We have all been impacted by our childhood experiences of the care we received and the care we went without. We have all been impacted by our childhood experiences with our parents and caregivers.

I do not mean to sit as a judge of all the parents who have gone before us, or of us who are learning something new. We are talking about how parenting relationships hurt children, and how at some points this is unavoidable.

No matter where you are in your mix of relationships, you are here, reading this book. This is one step further into the love you are already included in. It takes courage to keep taking one perfectly-imperfect step after the other. Each step counts.

As you read this book, you may find some parts stir up emotion. Please do keep in tune with yourself — your body and your feelings. If things inside of you start to feel potent, do what you need to do to take notice of this potency. Self-regulate, co-regulate, ask for help, talk your thoughts and feelings through, listen to some music, sit and think, cry, go for a walk… tune in.

> Let both the hopeful and the scary parts of this book resound through you.

Contemplative Questions:

How will you slow yourself down for a moment and feel some feelings about you and about your people?

How are you feeling about your story of being somebody's child?

If you are a parent, go easy on yourself. But still notice:

How do you feel about being someone's parent?

One of my favorite discoveries about attachment theory is that *"it is never too late."* You and I are both here because we are hopeful to understand love in a new way. As we gain more understanding of love we can participate in love, and sense more and more how completely we are included in the same heart of love as everyone else. From the cradle to the grave we are included, and from the cradle to the grave it is never too late to access the fullness of our belonging. Are you curious? Let's continue this discussion in our next chapter.

NEVER TOO LATE

From early infancy, it appears that our ability to regulate emotional states depends upon the experience of feeling that a significant person in our life is simultaneously experiencing a similar state of mind.
Daniel J. Siegel[1]

Our attachment story is a big part of our own unique story. A story that continues from the cradle to the grave, just as our yearning for *love-energy* continues from the time we were babies, until this very day, then from this day into our future.

It is never too late too learn to have loving ears for our sad songs, to have loving eyes for the parts of our story that are difficult to look at, to have a loving mind for all the parts of our story that have been written well and all the parts that have tragic plots —the twists and the turns. All of our inner experience began the day we were born, as our life unfolds our narrative continues to be written. This is why it is important we pay close attention to our inner loneliness, fear, flaws, and our defaults. It is common to see the term *inner child* introduced in conversations like this one. And of course, our *inner child* is of central importance to our cradle to the grave, *never too late* story. So, let's start to weave in this important part of who we are.

---

[1] Seigel, Daniel J., Hartzell, Mary (2013). *Parenting From The Inside Out: How a Deeper Self-Understanding Can Help You Raise Children Who Thrive.* TarcherPerigee; 10th Anniversary ed. Edition.

> It is never too late to believe our whole self is always included in the same heart of love as everyone else.

Knowing our *inner child* is a very important part of our love discovery and *it is never too late* to begin this internal process of discovering and knowing and all of our whole selves. We learn to know our whole self, we learn to love our whole self, we can then embody *self-love,* and, in turn, we are better able to know and experience *love-energy.* I often say to clients, this is your opportunity to be a wise good mother (or a wise good father, an uncle or aunt, a mentor, an older, wiser, loving comrade) to your *inner child.* As you hear your own *inner child*'s story, you can listen, you can come alongside this younger part of self. You can speak to your child the unique things you needed to hear in your young life, in your pain moments. I also ask clients to think of an image of themselves as a child.

Perhaps you have a photo of yourself as a child. I do. It was taken on my grandpa's farm, I have very blonde, very tousled hair. I am holding a kitten in a stranglehold and my shirt is scrunched up exposing my lovely belly (or "bally" as my child-self preferred to say).

What image comes to mind for you?

Can you picture it in your mind?

Even better, can you find this image?

Can you hold this photo in your hands, then frame it and place it somewhere where you can see it?

This image is your little you, and *your little you,* your *inner child,* needs you to hear your story with loving ears, to see your image with loving eyes, to know your own *inner child* with your loving mind.

> *To speak love to your inner child.*
>
> *To comfort them.*
>
> *To value them.*
>
> *To include them just the way they are.*
>
> *To be mindful of their chapter in your love story and*
>
> *To keep written the rest of your story.*

Cherishing the image of your younger self does something for you. Listening for their little voice does something too. Heck, having this photo displayed in your home, or office, or as the screensaver on your phone, having this photo in your line of sight does something.

Much of our inner pain is rooted in our young relationship experiences when we were not heard, not seen, not known. It is never too late to learn how to hear, see, and know all the parts of who we are. All the chapters of our own personal love story. All the parts of who we are and how we are, our whole self is included in our story. The more we love our whole self the more whole we become.

The more awareness we have for our love story, the more love assures us there is a great mass of love we are all included in. With this new way of being, and as time goes on we will know this more and more, it is *never too late* to discover our whole self is loved, lovable and loving.

Love is a part of our story from the cradle to the grave, it is *never too late*. Since our time in the womb until the day we are placed in the earth. All the parts of who we are on the inside, our way of being in relationship with ourselves and others will always have energy. No matter how much or how little insight we have into what *love-energy* is.

> It is never too late to refresh our knowledge of *Love's Energy*.

What might happen as we hope that it is *never too late* for us and our love discovery? Can we learn to hope for a new way of being in the world around us? We might discover that we can express our loving nature more freely. We might begin to love the unlovable parts of who we are, we might begin to know and care for our flaws and fears, to know and love even our *inner child*. We might begin to fully live in the glimmer of being a whole person, perfectly-imperfect and okay. Loved just the way we are.

Contemplative Question:

What is your love story?

How is your relationship with your *inner child?*

Take a moment to make your plan to track down a photo of you as a child. Schedule a time to get this photo and place it somewhere you will see it.

The next section of this book will expand further on how to practice *self-love*. Trusting our loving nature is hard business. You do not have to believe this just now but stay curious and let's continue our love conversation.

Tara Boothby

Love and Love's Energy

Tara Boothby

LOVING

Love and Love's Energy

LOVE FOR YOU & ME

"In hatred as in love, we grow like the thing we brood upon. What we loathe, we graft into our very soul." — Mary Ainsworth[1]

All of our ways of being in and out of relationships, all of our peopling ability with others is rooted in our core being: our whole self.

In this section called LOVING we will focus on our personhood. How we work our way into *self-love*, trusting *self-love* will transform our inner whole self and our relationships.

Are you ready to turn the page?

To ponder on your whole self?

To ponder on self-love?

---

[1] Ainsworth (Salter), Mary, Blehar, Mary C., Waters, Everett, Wall, Sally (1979). *Patterns of Attachment: A Psychological Study of the Strange Situation.* Routledge.

Love and Love's Energy

BEING BORN

I have a theory about childbirth. I am 98% sure I am right. I think when we are born, we think we are dying. I will venture even further and say being born is likely our first existential crisis.

Seriously, think about it:

> You are conceived and your little cells do their little cell things. Your little heart starts pumping. Your little organs start growing and your brain starts being. Your little arms and legs, your itty-bitty fingers and toes, your little eyeballs, and tiny lips, all spring forth with design. All of you is knit together in a cozy, warm, soft place with an all-inclusive package—your whole little world with its own rhythm. You are the star attraction. Then, one day, some earthquakes start rippling through your spectacular oasis. Things start getting weird! And squeezy!? Your normal world, the only world you have always known starts to feel dangerous. You feel unsafe. Frightened. And then you are forced to evacuate. Catapulted out of the one place you have always known!

Sitting at my table with my kids in the other room watching a cartoon, I imagine if the house were to start shaking and squishing, contracting, and I was forced out, pushed out, of my comfortable, mostly safe, definitely familiar, place. I know how I exist here. If all of a sudden the walls started moving and the room started squeezing me out of my home, I would definitely think I was dying (or living my best evangelical experience of the *Left Behind* movie).

I have to believe these little babies don't trust that a good thing is happening to them. All at once, they are pushed out through a small tunnel, and their food supply is cut off, they are cold, and their little minds realize being covered in slime is not as wonderful in this new place. To make matters more frightening, a bunch of gloved hands start to work at them, wiping at them, stretching them out, sucking goo out of their face. It makes sense the baby is about to lose all hope. They have been abducted to a worse reality.

> Ideally, unless there is a trauma of some sort, what comes next is something magical. They are placed on some kind of pillow. But wait, it's not a pillow. It's something very familiar. Then very, very familiar. It sounds like home. A homey beat drops and baby starts to settle. This is Mommy! This is the steady sound of Mommy's heart! This is Mommy's voice and all the glories that go with Mommy!

Mommy's body does an amazing cortisol chill out thing. Baby's body responds to Mommy's, they co-regulate. Baby can sense Mommy's joy and Daddy's echoes, and maybe even some other familiar voices, and this place starts to sound like home.[1] Baby's body calms and steadies and baby realizes baby is hungry. Instinctually baby finds its way to Mommy's breast, and then this place even starts to taste like home.[2]

---

[1] Queen's University (2003, May 13). Fetus Heart Races When Mom Reads Poetry: New Findings Reveal Fetuses Recognize Mother's Voice In-utero. www.sciencedaily.com/releases/2003/05/030513080440.htm.

[2] Le Leche League. Breastfeeding After Caesarean Birth. Llli.org/breastfeeding-info/breastfeeding-caesarean-birth/

In this first hour, the hour we call *"the magical hour,"* baby co-regulates with Mommy in a brand-new way as their skin touches and Mommy's heartbeat assures baby this place is still where baby belongs.[1] Baby may even co-regulate in a brand-new way with other people like Daddy. As baby presses heart-to-heart, skin to skin with Daddy, or Aunty, or Grandpa, or Sister, baby hears another safe heartbeat. Baby starts to find this new world is full of love. The love baby experiences calms baby. Baby realizes they are *alive*.[2]

The miracle of childbirth is another great reminder of how we see attachment in terms of life and death. From the moment we are born, we learn to cry for our mother in our darkest need. At birth, our survival depends on her finding us and caring for us. If we lost our birth mom, we could adapt and learn some other primary caregiver will meet our cries for help, we can learn to be soothed by a caregiver other than our biological mother. But we need a caregiver. Our infant life depends on it, literally.

Not all children experience the miracle of coregulation and breastfeeding in the first few hours or even days of their life for many reason. But from the very beginning of life it is never too late for attachment, and when medical emergencies are cared for, and mommy and baby find each other, their miracle begins. If it happens to be that mommy will not join in on baby's life, baby will begin their attachment story with other caregivers.

The magic of this first meeting between caregiver and child is our first proof of the power of love-energy. Infants that have increasing experiences of co-regulating relationships have more hope for loving relationships with new people throughout their

---

[1] Brimdyr, Kajsa: www.magicalhour.org.

[2] Neufeld, Gordon, Mate, Gabor (2006). Hold On To Your Kids: Why Parents Need To Matter More Than Peers. Ballentine Books.

lives.[1] But, as we have started to discuss, all caregivers will miss the mark at times. Eventually, every caregiver misses their baby's cries for help. Then time goes on. Babies turn into children who turn into teens who turn into adults. No matter the developmental stage they are at they have feelings and sometimes their feelings will show up in big ways. When parents lose their footing, and we often will, our child's anger toward us makes us feel like our worst fears about ourselves are all true.[2] We feel all our flaws, and we default as parents, we default in our relationship with our children just as we can default in all other relationships, because we are people. We don't want our children to see our fallibility. However, when we try to hide our flaws from our children, we often miss our child's need to co-regulate with us. And when we don't soothe their discomfort, they are left alone in their dysregulation.[3]

Even young children start to learn their own version of *"I belong alone."* Their lonely view of themselves may sound like:

> *"I am angry"; "I hurt Mommy"; "I am mean"; "I am too needy"; "No one helps me"; "No one cares"; "Being sad is bad"; "Hide"; "It's my fault"; "Love hurts"; "I am a brat"; "I am bad"; "Mommy loves my brother more than me"; "Daddy doesn't want to play with me"; "Big people are too busy to notice me"; "I can run away and no one will come for me"; "I am silly"; "I am hungry"; "I am tired"; "I am dirty"; "I*

---

[1] Powell, Bert, Cooper, Glen, Hoffman, Kent (2016). The Circle of Security: Enhancing Attachment In Early Parent-Child Relationships. The Guilford Press.

[2] Furrow, James L., Palmer, Gail, Johnson, Sue M., Faller, George, Palmer-Olsen, Lisa (2019). Emotionally Focused Family Therapy: Restoring Connection and Promoting Resilience. Routledge.

[3] Ainsworth (Salter), Mary, Blehar, Mary C., Waters, Everett, Wall, Sally (1979). Patterns of Attachment: A Psychological Study of the Strange Situation. Routledge.

am not enough"; "I am dumb"; "I am fat"; "I am slow"; "I don't fit in"; "No one likes me"; "No one will ever understand"; "I'm a joke"; "Life would be better without me"; "People won't miss me when I am gone"; and so on. The cycle repeats. The root of our flaws, these beliefs, start early.

It's hard to trust it is okay for us to be perfectly-imperfect when it comes to parenting. Yet, parents who are not at peace with being perfectly-imperfect don't know how to support their children to trust it is completely okay for them to be perfectly-imperfect kids.

Of course, we never lose the desire to do a good job of the importance job of being Mommy and Daddy. But we aim too high. We expect other people actually know what they are doing, or at least other parents know better than we do.

One of the easiest lies to get stuck in is 'parents should know what we are doing'. No parent knows. Not once in all my years of therapy have I ever met a parent that really knows what they are doing all the time, and neither do I. We are continually learning a new parenting plan, then, when we think we have it down and have figured out a strategy, our kids move into a new developmental stage or experience, and we have to adjust and readjust, and try new approaches— some of which won't work.

Parenting is always trial and error, but we need it to be fueled by love whenever possible. When we blunder, we need to offer *self-love* to ourselves knowing it is possible to find our way back to having loving ears, loving eyes, and a loving mind toward our kids. Our children learn from our modeling.[1]

---

[1] Neufeld, Gordon, Mate, Gabor (2006). Hold On To Your Kids: Why Parents Need To Matter More Than Peers. Ballentine Books.

When parents strategize to love our perfectly-imperfect selves and to love the perfectly-imperfect people around us, our children are watching. We are always modelling what love is to our children whether we are loving or not. Children discover love and *self-love* from the magic they experience in their relationship with their parents, or they do not.

We get to be perfectly-imperfect in every area of our lives, as people, as parents and even as someone's child. There is no need to cast blame. From the moment a child is born they are born for love. We are all born to give and receive love. Children naturally watch their parents to learn just this truth. Children see their parents model what is loving and what is not, and then they will do similar actions.

Our influence on the children around us has great impact. A baby is born a miracle, and they are born to experience the miracle of love. A baby is born, thinking it's dying, then experiences epic love. I do wish we could remember more about our participating in the miracle of creating a life, and the miracle of nurturing this life.

> What if we try to make *"magical hours"* outside of the delivery room? Mini moments of co-regulating, *magical moments*. Moments where we feel completely present in our own body and feel every ounce of love we have capacity to give, receive, and hold as we hold one other and are held by one other.
>
> What if we believe in the power of our own loving arms and we open our loving arms to other people? What if we start a *Coregulation Revival*?
>
> What if we do this often? If we hold abundant love inside ourselves and hug other people. What

if we get good at noticing our biological experience of co-regulation? If we stop "side hugging" and start intentionally practicing heart-to-heart hugs.

What if we do this as often as possible? If we, within emotionally safe relationships, become determined to participate in hugs, and more hugs, where we press our heart against another heart and intentionally *catch the beat* with each other?

We are all born into the same heart of love.

We are always included in love.

May we find where we have always belonged.

Contemplative Question (again, these questions are optional. But it is good to pause and consider all that you are learning in each section and chapter of this book):

What is your birth story and how has this impacted your love story?

And now, what about *self-love*? Let's find out in the next chapter.

Love and Love's Energy

SELF-LOVE

"The beginning of love is to let those we love be perfectly themselves, and not to twist them to fit our own image."
Thomas Merton[1]

Love inspires us to become intimately acquainted with our own unique, messy, whole self.

Hiding your mess does not work.

Twisting your mess does not work.

It doesn't work for you, and it doesn't work for me.

We need to know our mess. If we twist ourselves to fit in, we will run the risk of requiring the same of others. If we ignore the mess inside, the mess is still there carrying influence. Love inspires us to love ourselves as much as love inspires us to love others. Without loving ourselves, our mess will inspire our default way of being, and then we are at increasing risk of living on autopilot when we lack *self-love*.

Remember, our defaults aren't all bad. Like our flaws, we are not trying to omit our defaults, we are not trying to omit any part of who we are. As we love ourselves, we are empowered to know ourselves, and are better equipped to practice *self-love*. The less *self-love* we practice the more we aim to hide our mess, the more we fall back to our defaults. Without *self-love* we strategize to develop methods to cover up our inner

---

[1] Merton, Thomas (2002). No Man Is an Island. Harper Collins (republished).

flaws and fear. It is hard to trust we can love ourselves, so we protect ourselves by our defaults.

Lacking a *self-love* practice and instead covering our whole self by defaults is serious business. And it can have a serious impact on us and our relationships.

> Default behaviors we love to hate include: *being mean, being compulsive, being neurotic, authoritarian, rule focused, being violent, being contemptuous, having to be right, disrespecting boundaries, coercing affection, getting in the way of other's personal growth and goals, making things about us and our needs, martyring, neglecting, avoiding, ignoring, humiliating, mocking, being overly logical, being task oriented or functional, giving in, appeasing, blaming, being afraid, weak, fake, scary, scared, abusive, racist, absent, ashamed, unloving,* the list continues.

> Default behaviors we hate to love include: *people pleasing, perfectionism, codependency, overachieving, being an emotional doormat, being a yes person, going with the flow, not having an opinion, staying off the radar, peacekeeping, being pious, being informed and aware, being helpful, taking over, taking on other people's problems, charism, being charming, putting on an act, and again,* the list continues.

How detrimental it is for us to live without *self-love*.

> *Self-love is about seeing our flaws and loving ourselves anyhow.*
>
> *Self-love is about finding our way of being our whole self*

Without having to put on our defaults.
Self-love is us loving our mess,
Without twisting ourselves to fit.
All of our ways of being,
All of our story is included.

When we choose to be authentic as whole people, we are challenged to become acquainted with how *self-love* resounds throughout our very being. When we practice *self-love* we learn we can be authentic with our love for other people. Eventually we love ourselves to a point where we are less inclined to hide our whole self, we are less inclined to invent defaults to cover our flaws and fear, because we have more faith that we are okay to be perfectly-imperfect.

> When we practice *self-love*, we will be better able to practice *love-energy*, to see the moments of love we give to others, as well as the moments of love given to us. What a beautiful truth!

Humanity is designed to be experienced within relationships. We continue to hold the gravity of this life and death longing for attachment experience our entire lives. *Self-love* is paramount to our self-discovery, recovery, and healing — a beautiful beginning as we unveil the grander mass of love that we already belong to.

I love me and so I love you.
Self-love is not selfish;
It is not self-indulgence,
It is not superficial,
It is not a luxury.

Self-love is love-energy.

Self-love is an inside job, and it draws us further into the

Vastness of the love that is all around us.

Our love for our whole self is the beginning of where we belong.

From the source of our self-love, all love flows.

This is another good place to take a pause. To let your thoughts come and go.

Let them pass over this new valuing of *self-love*.

Contemplative Questions:

Do you have old constructs about *self-love* to throw out?

How do you sense *self-love* resounds through you?

How can you discipline yourself to increase *self-love*?

What questions do you have for yourself about *self-love*?

A couple other terms that pair up with *self-love* are *self-compassion* and *empathy*. These terms can be over used in the psychology and self-help world. However, they are deeply valuable concepts for us to be curious about. *How do self-compassion and empathy come to play with self-love?* Let's explore this next.

SELF-COMPASSION & EMPATHY

"If you talk to a man in a language he understands, that goes to his head. If you talk to him in his language, that goes to his heart."
Nelson Mandela[1]

Will you learn to speak a language that goes straight to your own heart?

Self-love is rooted in compassionate conversations with ourselves. These internal loving conversations are the source from which we learn what empathy for others truly is. Without self-compassion, we cannot really offer empathy. Empathy without self-compassion is a default. It's false.

Self-compassion is accepting ourselves with awareness of our flaws and aloneness. True empathy is picking up all of our messy self, and still reaching out to heap love on someone else. We empathize with ourselves by loving and accepting our whole self. We learn to have compassion for our whole self, flaws and all, and then we come alongside others to love them as whole people.

| Self-compassion says: *what's so bad about me?*

It takes great perseverance to keep reaching out to offer love, even when other people may not offer this back to us. Some people will not be capable of accepting our offers because they are too uncertain of

[1] Noah, Trevor (2016). Born A Crime: Stories From a South African Childhood. Random House.

their own inner state. Some people will completely reject us. Some people will struggle then concede. Others will be more like us in that they practice *self-love*, so they also know the disciple of self-compassion. They will revel in our efforts, and the energy between us will be a volley of love. As proof, self-compassion will help us move through whatever occurs in our relationships as we love ourselves and love other people.

> Self-compassion and empathy go hand in hand.

We show up for ourselves first. We have compassion for our perfectly-imperfect self. We love ourselves as whole people, then we learn how to do this for others; this is empathy. We love others as whole people without deciding their worthiness of our loving.

Self-compassion and empathy remind us we are truly included in the same heart of love as everyone else. We are all included. Without having compassion to love ourselves we are limited in so many ways. Self-compassion challenges us to love ourselves without evaluating our own worthiness. Self-compassion leads us to embody *self-love* more and more. It is enough to stop here, but through empathy we help others discover that they too are included in the same heart of love as we are.

> *Self-love* is authenticated by self-compassion and empathy.

Contemplative Questions:

Will you learn to speak a language that goes straight to your own heart?

Will you learn to speak a language that goes straight to the heart of others?

How will self-compassion expand your empathy for yourself and others?

Self-love is not the beginning of our love story, but it plays a key role in the mystery of how we interact with ourselves and others. *Self-love* influences our ability to love and interact with others. *Self-love* is paramount to our internal working model, as such, how we love ourselves will positively or negatively impact how we see ourselves and others.

Love and Love's Energy

THE MYSTERY OF SELF-LOVE

"Relationships early in life may shape the very neural structures that create representations of experience and allow a coherent view of the world: Interpersonal experiences directly influence how we mentally construct reality."
Daniel J. Siegel[1]

We have all lost out in relationships at one time or another. This is not a fatal defect of our collective humanity; neither is this the cause of an unloving God. Relationships are hard. No parent gets it right for their children 100% of the time, just like no romantic partner, family member, teacher, pastor, politician, boss, colleague, or friend gets it right all the time. In fact, it is argued by some of the most notable attachment theorists that perfect parenting is not only impossible but may prove detrimental to attachment bonding[2]. We may generalize these research findings to all other key relationships in our lives. Why might perfect parenting be detrimental? Well, a child who experiences a perfect parent will not have the experience of seeing a *stronger, wiser, other* process through noticing their mistake, and offering repair to this child. (Stronger, wiser, other is a phrase coined by John Bowlby. It is his concise summation of the root attributes we seek certainty for in our caregivers).[3]

---

[1] Seigel, Daniel J. (2020). *The Developing Mind: How Relationships and the Brain Interact to Shape Who We Are.* The Guilford Press.

[2] Powell, Bert, Cooper, Glen, Hoffman, Kent (2016). *The Circle of Security: Enhancing Attachment In Early Parent-Child Relationships.* The Guilford Press.

[3] Bowlby, John. (1988). *A Secure Base: Parent-Child Attachment and*

This is not only true for children but for all of us, we observe the people who love us getting it wrong for us, and then see them processing through how to repair this with us.

We are not meant to be perfect in relationships with others. We are meant to be ourselves alongside others who are being themselves. All of us perfectly-imperfect individuals alongside one another.

> We are all people: sometimes we hurt others and sometimes they hurt us.

Relationships hurt at times. When we keep believing there is some perfect formula for being a person that erases our flaws and transforms our fear of being alone, we are never satisfied. Thus, we are always afraid when we get nicked by relational pain. When we are walloped by toxic relationships, we may wonder if all hope for us is lost. These experiences lend us to a negative view of ourselves and others. Our proof is compelling. It is easy to believe the worst about ourselves.

We naturally wonder: *Why is my experience of love limited?* We wonder when we see other people receiving the kind of love we ourselves are not receiving. We worry that others understand love in a way we have no knowledge of and we don't understand love the way others do. Of course, we wonder *"why me?"* We believe we are unincluded. We feel singled out. We are prone to create theories as to why hurt has left us solo yet again.[1]

Healthy Human Development. Basic Books.

> We cannot escape relationships with people.
> We cannot escape relationship with ourselves.
> We believe we can escape a relationship with God, but we cannot do that either.

Even if we are isolated in the depths of the forest, we are all still somebody's child. Our relationships from the past are always carried with us and are internal to us, no matter where our feet may carry us. Even if we can fly to the moon and live a deserter's life, we cannot escape ourselves, or the energy experiences we have shared with others. *love-energy* and neglect energy both travel with us.

> *When we view ourselves negatively,*
>
> *This view sticks with us.*
>
> *When we view others negatively,*
>
> *This view sticks with us.*
>
> *We need a transformation.*

What might we do to transform our old negative view of ourselves and other people? A simple thing we can do is notice, as often as possible, when we are getting it wrong for ourselves and our people and repair these times with intuitiveness and sensitivity. In as much, notice the times we are hurt by others then wonder about these hurts. Hurting others is going to happen. Being hurt by others is going to happen. Making sense of these hurts is valuable; and it is a choice. We can choose to make sense of hurt.

Being brave to notice our errored beliefs and behaviors will challenge us to see and experience our emotional life differently. There are no bad feelings. Our uncomfortable emotions truly are signals to us that something is going on inside. Feeling hurt is worth noticing. Our hurt is going to help us uncover our version of *"I belong alone"* because our hurt will bring us to know our fear, if we are willing. It is going to help us get curious about what we are thinking and believing about our flaws. Our hurt challenges us to see our view of ourselves, of others, of the world around us, and of God.

Wherever we look, whatever we see, is influenced by our beliefs about our own identity, and our beliefs about the identity of the people around us. This is why when someone is doing a little bit better than us many of us have a hard time cheering them on. A strange parallel is we also find it hard to see a vulnerable person in pain, to see the underdog being kicked while they are down. We struggle to understand how to view other people in light of how we view ourselves.

Any time someone has a moment of being *"something special,"* it can be hard for the rest of us. Most of us do not know what to do when we touch our own jealousy. We are taught being jealous is wrong, because of this we feel flawed and try to hide our jealousy. We get judgmental of those who are excelling. We get critical, or maybe we martyr our own *"not good enough."*

> What if we learn to see jealousy is also a signal, like hurt, something for us to notice and counsel ourselves through? Then jealousy is not a bad feeling; it is a helpful signal.

> There is something about being in the spotlight. Whether we are comfortable with having the light of attention shone on us or not, when others take notice of us, we want to be seen favorably. Could our uncomfortable jealousy be reminding us that we long to be admired? Could our jealousy be reminding us that we are grateful to have simplicity in our lives that someone in the

spotlight may never know? We will not know if we never get slow and listen to our inner voice.

When we do something flawed and receive a sideways glance, we are going to feel uncomfortable. Feeling uncomfortable is not bad. However, most of us feel an uncomfortable feeling and our inner dialogue takes over. Perhaps your inner dialogue sounds something like this....

> *"I feel bad, I look bad, I am bad. There must be something fundamentally wrong with me. Therefore, I need to cover these fatal flaws about who I am or be banished to never experience the love everyone else is more deserving of. If people figure out how flawed I truly am, I will be all alone."* This is a negative view of self and others.

You have your own battle with not being known as you truly are, and so do I. And yet, we still hide our whole self from the world around us. We long to be accepted, but we are unsure this is an acceptable longing, because everyone else is working as hard to hide their flaws. Other people are seemingly so much better at life. This influences us. We learn to run toward attention or run away from it.

Somehow, we see being viewed positively as a requirement of our survival. Being seen favorably is preferable, but not always possible. Without love for others, we need to protect ourselves from their shine. Other's shine becomes unbearable, utterly intimidating. *"I see you in the spotlight and I feel left out."* Other people are going to outshine us at times. We are allowed to feel jealous. Noticing our jealousy and being brave enough to talk to our jealousy is a new way of being.

When we sidestep our emotions, jealousy and all the other ones, we miss the opportunity to love ourselves through our wobbly moments. The aim is to love even our wobbly bits. *Self-love* leads us to a positive view of ourselves, which leads us to a positive view of other people.

Learning that feeling uncomfortable is not bad is a good first step. When we make friends with what is uncomfortable we see our feelings for what they are: a signal. We learn to be on friendly terms with our emotions, and we are better able to hear their signals. We have more valuable conversations with ourselves about ourselves. Our feelings mentor us. We realize our feelings are vital to our *self-love* and the energy that drives our view and love for others.

> Learning to see our feelings as an old friend, we greet them as they show up and start a conversation: *"Hello, hurt, what do you have to say today?"*

We begin to hear, see and know our emotional signals and their contribution to our grander internal conversation; this discovery is essential to our *self-love;* we discover how to love ourselves just as we are.

We are people—people like everybody else.

We will continue to make mistakes.

We will make poor choices.

We are perfectly-imperfect.

We are people—people like everybody else. And,

We are pure-of-heart.

People deserving of love.

People included in the same heart of love.

We become determined to know these truths, then

Our beliefs about ourselves and those around us transform.

Loving ourselves and loving others are beautiful mysteries to discover. Mystery is an important word to use here. Mystery is uncomfortable and amazing. Living without mystery is not a way to live. Without mystery discovery is limited. But life is mysterious, and this mystery is an energy all its own. Our inner world seems mysterious, and *self-love* naturally leads us to wonder about our inner mystery. We are wonderful mysteries. The mystery of our inner world compels us. Our own mystery and being open to the mystery of others compliments how we view ourselves and others with love.

> *Self-love* transforms our mystery. Without discovering the beauty of our own mystery, we will always struggle to discover how awesomely mysterious others are. The mystery of *love-energy* is a revelation. Mystery draws us into the vastness of supernatural love.
>
> Our human relationships are best experienced when they mirror love. *Self-love* holds the mirror. The mystery of *love-energy* is seeing others in our own reflection and seeing our own reflection in others.

The mystery of *self-love* and *love-energy* is how the story of honoring the value of ourselves and others unfolds. Deep down everyone yearns to know someone sees us, really sees us. To trust we are forgiven before we admit to what we have done, to be smiled at, to get a laugh, to be able to speak about our mistakes and still be accepted, to be anxious and struggle with not liking ourselves, to find successes and to be excited about our success, to be grateful for being exactly who we are, to have trust for praise, admiration, contentment, commitment— to experience all of this in the context of relationship and have someone say, *"you're okay."*

Contemplative questions:

How have you viewed yourself and others?

Will you let love influence how you see yourself?

Will you let love influence how you see others?

And what may be the flip side of *self-love*? Or, at least, what do we expect is the opposite of *self-love*? Let's explore this in our next chapter.

SHAME, GUILT, HUMILIATION

"We cultivate love when we allow our most vulnerable and powerful selves to be deeply seen and known, and when we honor the spiritual connection that grows from that offering with trust, respect, kindness and affection... Shame, blame, disrespect, betrayal, and the withholding of affection damage the roots from which love grows. Love can only survive these injuries if they are acknowledged, healed and rare."
Brené Brown[1]

Whichever one screams loudest in your ear, whether that be shame, guilt, or humiliation, pay attention. It is good to determine which exact word is yours; or if it is some other synonym.

It is likely that someone shamed or blamed you when you were really little. Someone pointed out your flaws and laughed in your face when you were a child. Someone pinned you to the ground and tickle tortured you for being you when you were small; you have not forgotten it. Now, when your behavior is flawed, you can shame yourself. Your body remembers how to make you feel small in comparison to your shame, blame, and humiliation. You look in the mirror and, all on your own, you ignite all of your personal flavor of self-condemnation.

---

[1] Brown, Brené (2010). The Gifts of Imperfection: Let Go of Who You Think You're Supposed to Be and Embrace Who You Are. Hazelden.

> Shaming, blaming, and humiliating is always unloving. It is never *"just a joke"* to lord someone's faults over them, especially a child. There is nothing funny about pointing out what is shameful about someone. This behavior is always cruel. This behavior is always unloving.

Some of us are so well practiced at living with shame, guilt, and humiliation that we don't even need to make big mistakes anymore. We are experts on our own flaws and when they show up, we grind ourselves into the ground, feeling our version of *"I belong alone"* and jumping into our default shame response plan. When we feel all these terrible feelings, we are not trying to deny our *pure-of-heartness,* we just don't understand how to reconcile our shame. We use defaults to escape feeling the unfathomable cruelness of other people and our own unfathomable cruelness of self-loathing.

And it is not always other people using shame against us. Sometimes when we touch our own shame, we will quickly jump to point out someone else's shame. We see someone else's shame and point it out to protect ourselves from anyone realizing how similar our flawed shame is to that which someone has shamefully been exposed for. We are truly trying to care for ourselves, but at the cost of shaming another.

Shame, guilt, and humiliation are a part of our strategy to cover our inner fear and flaws, they are ways that we default. At times we use shame as a weapon, and at other times we feel deeply troubled and riddled by our own fear of shame.

Shame makes us feel defectively alone. Of course, we try to protect ourselves from feeling this way. We are simply trying to take care of ourselves without having to risk showing another person how damaged we are, especially when we have already learned our damage is shameful, worthy of critique, and humiliating to our identity. But hiding our whole self is no identity at all.

Unlike other uncomfortable feelings, shame, guilt, and humiliation are almost always given to us by others. Someone purposely figured out one of our flaws then explicitly called negative attention to it. People do this to feel powerful. We do this to other people to feel powerful.

> Increased experiences of shame, guilt, and humiliation, lead to increased fear that we are destined to be all alone if we do not cover up what we believe is defective about us. It is a never-ending shame cycle unless we learn to see our own unique shame pattern for what it is.

Shame inspires us to strategize to hide our flaws. If we pay attention shame is often at the root of some common defaults.

> *Workaholism* could seem helpful, or taking a deep dive into *self-help* literature and its culture may seem soothing, or *giving your absolute all* to absolutely everyone, or *obsessing* on the one skill you know you are good at, or *taking extreme risks*, or *numbing out, running fast, running away, stopping any sort of movement, or dissociating*, and so on.

> And if you listen closely, you hear the beliefs shame enforce: *"If I was only perfect"*; *"If I was*

> *popular"; "If I was successful... aloof, tough, sexy, smart, funny, or meaner"; "If I could growl"; "If I could speak up"; "If I could shut up" or, or, or...*

Then what? Then nothing, literally nothing. We are still left feeling *alone*. Covering our painful shame does nothing to remedy our pain.

Like our other emotional experiences, when shame, guilt, and humiliation run wild, when they are unchecked inside of us, our defaults always take over. These painful experiences evoke a mix of some of the worst feelings. But there are no bad feelings, right? Right! Our feelings are valuable signals for us to learn to listen to.

> When we are courageous to notice where shame shows up in our day-to-day life, the old stories of where shame became unruly will start to be heard by us. Shame is a key to our past.

We are going to feel pain when we notice our shame and speak to it. Shame is worth paying attention to. As adults, when our shame shows up, and we let it advise us, it can teach us about the stories of its origin. In each of our brains shame has a collection of stories that span over our entire lifetime.

We are just touching on the surface of this very important subject. Shame may not be the true opposite of *self-love*, but shame definitely distracts us from loving ourselves, and it definitely is a weapon when we use it against others.

Contemplative Questions:

Do you know your stories of shame, guilt, and humiliation?

Which word feels most potent to you? Or is there a better synonym?

Do you know the voice of shame?

How does it sound? Is it male or female? How do you visualize it?

Take a moment and listen for this voice.

When we first start to listen for the voice of shame, or other uncomfortable feelings, they will probably say something awful. Don't fret. Keep reading. The following chapters will help you to consider how to *tune in* to yourself.

Love and Love's Energy

A NOTE ON VULNERABILITY

"Avoidance will make you feel less vulnerable in the short run, but it will never make you less afraid."
Brené Brown[1]

In the early 2000s, in the lower mainland of British Columbia, I was a clinical addictions counsellor. I believe the 12-step curriculum is one of the greatest tools we have for life recovery. A golden tool of the Anonymous meetings is the serenity prayer, which has a line:

> *"That we may be reasonably happy in this life and supremely happy with [higher power] forever in the next."[2]*

This line makes me believe we've gotten things mixed up. When we keep pursuing *"supreme happiness"* in this life, then we start to believe all we have to look forward to is being *"reasonably happy"* with God in the next life.

Can you hear a little voice inside of you asking:

> *"Am I really happy?"* *"What the heck is supremely happiness anyway?"* As you touch these questions, do you notice your brain tugging you toward

---

[1] Brown, Brené (2015). *Rising Strong: The Reckoning, The Rumble. The Revolution.* Random House.

[2] Niebuhr, Reinhold (1941). *"The Serenity Prayer"* Obituary. New York Herald Tribune.

> solutions of how *"you too can create your own supreme happiness!"*

Yet again these are your old automatic negative thoughts working at you to pull you away from being vulnerable with yourself. You are not alone. We all avoid vulnerability at times, most of us avoid it often. How do you avoid vulnerability?

> *Do you look like you have it all together? Are you ultra-confident? Are you the life of the party? Are you sweet as pie? Are you an open book? Do you read every book? Do you make and break plans? Are you the supreme hostess? Are you a bad ass? Are you the ultimate volunteer? Selfless always? The leader of all things community? The last one to leave the office at night? The ever-doting parent? A gym rat? A lay pastor? A jack of all trades? A Houdini? Perfect in religion? An ultra-meditator? How do you protect yourself from your fear of being exposed?*

I want to affirm to you that vulnerability is not putting ourselves at risk with other people, vulnerability is getting really real with our inside world, falling into our inside fear and flaws, to eventually find all of the parts of who we are, and then to love all the parts of who we are, as we are.

| Vulnerability is our co-pilot if we allow it to be.

Vulnerability sweeps us up and pushes us over the edge of our chasm of self, then it lets us fall until we learn to fly. It takes us deeper and deeper into our experience of self. It makes us face whether we will learn to trust ourselves. Vulnerability asks us to authentically learn *self-love*.

Vulnerability is a great example of how our feelings advise us. Vulnerability signals us. It is a tangle of emotions and perceptions, and it is signaling us to more valuable truths about who we are. Vulnerability feels uncomfortable, because it is complex. Yet, when we learn to be skillful with our vulnerability, we grow to use it in emotionally safe ways.

> Vulnerability reveals to us that life is beautiful as it is. It longs to teach us we will feel great peace as we learn to pursue *to be reasonably happy in this life.*

There is a fragrant romance that will unfold between us and vulnerability as we venture with it. Vulnerability is a beautiful dance partner, bold, gentle, with vibrant complexity and effortless movement. We are out of our league when it comes to this increasing romance with vulnerability, but as we step into the dance of it all, we let ourselves be swept up, then swept up again, it feels more and more that we are right where we have always belonged.

Will you let vulnerability be one more beautiful element in your story of unfolding love?

Vulnerability cradles us and hears our voice. Just as,

Vulnerability holds the voices and the stories of the people in our lives.

Vulnerability springs from the source of love that we already belong to.

Thibaut, John W. (1986). The Social Psychology of Groups. Routledge.

Contemplative Questions:

How have you experienced vulnerability's fragrant romance in your life?

How have you experienced moments of vulnerability sweeping you over the edge and further into the depths of who you are, good and bad?

Vulnerability can help us make peace with ourselves, even the things we worry are bad about us. In the world of psychology we try not to use the word *"bad."* But there are times when we do feel *bad*, and there are things about our personhood that we do worry are *bad*. Now, we are learning that making peace with all of who we are, the good and the bad, that this is a part of our process of *self-love*.

THE GOOD AND THE BAD DOG

"The reasonable man adapts himself to the world: the unreasonable one persists in trying to adapt the world to himself."
George Bernard Shaw[1]

There is a common American Indian folklore about two dogs which live inside of us.

Let's imagine a scene from years gone by. An Indigenous chief and elders of the community take a group of young braves for a rites of passage ceremony. The boys are sitting around a fire, they are cooking some game they have killed during the day's hunt. The boys understand the seriousness of the time they are sharing with their elders, they know when they return to their people group, they will be seen as brave men.

The older, wiser men join the circle around the fire. The men share stories and wisdoms from their tradition. The elders speak in turn and the boys listen. Some stories evoke joy and laughter. Some carry the seriousness of caring for weaker community members, some speak of the duty of family. All at once the chief gestures for his turn to speak. The boys and elders fall silent.

---

[1] Bernard Shaw, George (2001). Man and Superman. Penguin Classics (republished).

> The chief says: *"Inside of each of you is a good dog and a bad dog, you decide which one you will feed."*[1]

There is a good and bad dog inside of each one of us. What feeds the good dog and what feeds the bad dog? The food each animal eats is the content of our daily lives—our good and bad feelings, our good and bad thoughts, our good and bad behaviors, what we view as flawed about us and what we view as desirable.

How big is the bad dog in comparison to the good dog? When people first notice their inner dogs, the bad dog is usually huge in comparison to the good dog.

> Both our good and bad dogs belong to us. We get to keep both. Although our bad dog may have grown fat and strong and big, we prove ourselves safe to this big, strong, mean dog. We learn to tame our bad dog. We learn the foods that cause our bad dog to grow sick from power, we instead nourish both of our dogs with what is good, we help both of our dogs to feel loved by us. We love our whole selves without regard for what is *good* and what is *bad*.

We approach all of the parts of who we are with loving ears, loving eyes, and a loving mind. We will struggle with loving the *good* parts of who we are at times, at other times we will struggle with loving the parts we deem as *bad*.

---

[1] Folklore.

Contemplative Questions:

What is the story of the good and bad dog in your life?

How have you used the terms *"good"* and *"bad"* to evaluate yourself in ways that have done you harm?

What causes your bad dog to grow sick from power?

How do you nourish the good parts of who you are as much as the bad?

There are many reasons and ways we can feel bad about who we are. Finding effective ways to love ourselves just the way we are is possible. The next chapter explores one of my favorite metaphors and clinical tools that I have developed in working with clients.

Love and Love's Energy

THE MAGIC MAGNET

"The most beautiful thing we can experience is the mysterious. It is the fundamental emotion which stands at the cradle of true art and true science. He who knows it not, no longer wonders, no longer feels amazement, is as good as dead. A snuffed-out candle."
Michael Green[1]

Our whole body is talking to us. Our physical body, our emotions, our thoughts, our memories, our behaviors—there is a lot of story inside of us to learn. Not to unlearn. To learn. Trying to leave it all behind, trying to undo the past, to grieve it and say goodbye to it, is a lie. Your whole self is included as is mine. We are completely included in the fullness of our identity, not in part.

You are learning to listen in to you. To hear yourself and to understand yourself. To see yourself; to know yourself and your mess. The more you know you, the more you can attune to your own self, and then the more you can do the same for others. We are discovering the energy of love.

With this love discovery we have more and more inspiration to help ourselves understand our inner fear. We understand that we have things we admire about who we are and things we worry are flawed. We also have a story we tell ourselves to justify the ways we feel rejected and to justify the behaviors we use to self-

---

[1] Green, Michael (2013). Quantum Physics and Ultimate Reality: Mystical Writings of Great Physicists. Amazon Kindle Direct Publishing.

preserve. This is a lot of work. With *self-love* we can hope to find a simpler way.

One of my favorite things to teach people is the power of *the magic magnet*! This is an amazing tool to help you on your *self-love* journey. Ready or not, let's do this!

> Right now, in my hand I am holding a magic magnet. I trust the powers of this magnet because for the past twenty years, it has always worked with the people I have turned it on. As you sit there reading this line, I am turning my magnet toward you. Can you see it in my hand? I am holding it and pointing it right at you. Through the pages of this book, it is pulling at you. I am going to use this magnet to pull all of the negative stuff off of you: *shame, anxiety, sadness, your negative view of self, your version of alone, the people pleasing, the faking good, the excellence, your mess, all of the words, all of the stories, all of the sad stuff, bad stuff, hurt stuff, and whatever else comes with it*. The magnet is pulling really hard. Let it.
>
> As all this mess is pulled off of you, I am going to drop it about two feet from you onto the floor. Look at it there. Really see it. Take a moment, or two, and really notice how it feels to have a bit of separation from all that has been pulled off of you.
>
> You need to know I not only have a magic magnet, but I also have a magic wand. I have put my magnet down and picked up my wand. I am reaching through the pages as best I can, and I am flipping and swirling my wand over your pile of mess, which is transforming into something: *a*

person, a character, a weather system. It could be anything: a demon, a tornado, the Tasmanian devil, a cartoon character, a policeman, a tiger, a black hole, an old lady, a war lord, a shadow of you, anything. What do you see? What became of your pile of mess?

As your mess takes form, listen to it. Does it sound familiar? There is a great chance the voice you hear is the same voice you heard in one of the previous chapters when you were listening for the voice of shame. Maybe not, but the mess is all stuck together and it usually shares one voice, or similar mirrors of one voice, at least at the start.

As you look at the mess and see it for what it is, what name will you give it? Here are some names I have heard over the years: *"Black cat"*; *"The demon"*; *"The monster"*; *"Squeaker"*; *"Fatso"*; *"Darth Vader"*; *"Hate"*; *"Addict"*; *"Homophobe"*; *"The truth"*; *"He-who-shall remain-nameless"*; *"The all-seeing eye"*; *"Death"*; *"Fucked up"*; *"Tornado"*; *"Dark lord"*; *"The thing"*; *"It"*; *"Evil"*; *"The bad dog."* At this beginning point this mess usually has a very ominous nature and a name to suit. What will you call your mess?

This is the beginning of many important conversations. The first conversation is so mighty a person's relationship with their mess may be utterly transformed, but we will have many conversations with our mess. As we go on, we will trust ourselves more, to the point we trust our mess belongs with us, we care for our mess and every nuance of it. What we have decided was ominous now becomes our correspondent, and eventually an advisor of sorts. Communication with our mess is difficult at the start, this is a budding relationship, it takes effort. Listening, learning, questioning, collaborating, challenging what is untrue, understanding our good intention behind our mess.

Our mess, now known by the name we give it, is included. We converse with it. It is a battle to start. But a helpful relationship can develop. We learn to love our mess and soothe our mess. Our mess belongs in our whole self.

Looking at our inner mess is vulnerable. Speaking with our inner mess is increasingly vulnerable. We have done a lot of vulnerable questioning thus far on our journey together. But we know this is important because vulnerability deepens our *self-love*.

Contemplative Questions:

What is your image of your mess?

What will you call this part of yourself?

> The next time you have concern that your mess has gotten you hooked into a negative way of being, or your defaults have taken over here are a few questions you might go through:

What do I see?

What is the event, person, or memory that has caused my mess to flare up?

What do I feel?

What do I think?

What do I do?

What do I actually want or need?

A simple and helpful line of questioning. This is something we can practice as often as we like, even daily if we choose. The more we communicate with our inner whole self, the better we hear, see, and know our whole self, messy parts and all. But what about the parts of our story that are very, very complicated? What about our trauma?

Love and Love's Energy

A NOTE ON TRAUMA

"Real life, even in its suffering, is much more deeply rewarding than imagined life."
William Paul Young[1]

The impact of trauma is not easy to predict. Some big traumas hit us on a small scale, and some small traumas hit us on a big scale. Trauma is subjective. We make general assumptions about what will hit someone harder, but trauma is individual to the beholder.

Healing is not about getting rid of parts of ourselves or our story. There is no "cancel culture" in this inside process. Our whole self is worthy of *self-love*, including our trauma.

You may not want to know certain things about yourself. It is normal to hide certain flaws or old wounds deep down inside; it is normal to hide your trauma. It might be too daring to believe you will be capable of bringing your whole self along with you. Some of us have experienced horrendous things at the hands of others, and even at the hands of ourselves.

Our bodies have a way of keeping us in pace with the items of our story we are working through, but we also need to be mindful to keep in tune with this internal pace.[2] We learn to check in with ourselves and our pace

---

[1] Young, Wm. Paul (2017). Lies We Believe About God. Atria Books.

[2] Van der Kolk, Bessel (2014). The Body Keeps The Score: Brain, Mind, and Body in the Healing of Trauma. Viking Press.

of dealing with what is traumatic for us, so we do not become overwhelmed. We can learn to become alert to this process, the alternative is that we may get flooded by our trauma and kick into autopilot, which is not a place we want to be.

Remember grieving the pain you have endured is valuable. Love yourself as you grieve your trauma and lean on someone else who is emotionally safe. Let this someone bear witness to your trauma story. Allow them to love you as you grieve. Let *self-love* and the *love-energy* of another person mingle and pour over your trauma story.

> Your trauma deserves your loving ears, loving eyes, and your loving mind to turn toward it.

If you are beginning your trauma discovery, it is good to consider sharing your story with a trained mental health professional, someone who can make sense of what has been traumatic for you. Anytime you touch a trauma place, it is okay, it is even good, to slow down, take a breath, and find what methods best keep you grounded. Trauma most often causes us to lose our footing, but there is healing on the other side.

Contemplative Questions:

Where are you at with your trauma discovery?

How do you keep in pace with soothing your trauma?

Are you ready to find out what to do with your sorrowful trauma? If you need to take a breath, or two, before you move on do. Keep in pace with you as best as you can. I hope you find the next chapter is another helpful tool, particularly for strategizing with your trauma.

A LITTLE ROOM IN OUR BRAIN

"The amygdala in the emotional center sees and hears everything that occurs to us instantaneously and is the trigger point for the fight or flight response."
Daniel Goleman[1]

Let's suppose in our brain a small child is watching television. This child sits in our brain's emotion center, our amygdala.[2] When something happens in the world around us our little child flips to the TV channel that seems most fitting. If something reminds them of our trauma, our child will flip to our trauma channel. On this channel, we have years and years of programming, years and years of whatever trauma each of us have endured as individuals.

In this little room, called the amygdala, sits our little child. This child is like any other child, but they are our very own *inner child*. As they watch whatever programming they want, they are unsupervised, until we notice them. They turn the TV to the station of their choosing, and they turn the volume up as loud as they want. They control the remote control. They turn the TV off and on.

---

[1] Goleman, Daniel (1995). *Emotional Intelligence: Why It Can Matter More Than IQ.* Bantam Books.

[2] Goleman, Daniel (1995). Emotional Intelligence: Why It Can Matter More Than IQ. Bantam Books.

Can you see this room? Can you see your child?

> The volume of the TV echoes through our mind. When the trauma channel is on, trauma echoes through our mind. We visualize the images the child is watching as we hear the content of the stories. Our child does not mean to do harm. They are feeling all our feelings and trying to find a story to help us to make sense of these feelings. The child flips through the channels and eventually says: *"Ha! This feels right! I feel like watching this!"*
>
> This child belongs to us. They may not know it. They may not feel they belong with anyone at all. And so, we want to come to them. To come and sit with them in our little room in our mind, our little amygdala. We take time to notice and understand our *inner child* and we become more aware of how our child feels about themselves, about us, and about the content they are flipping through.
>
> Sometimes there is a great deal of programming that a certain channel plays in our mind for a very long time. Sometimes the programming is so compelling we cannot figure out how to turn the channel off again. No matter how hard we try, or how many times we have turned it off in the past, sometimes the channel won't change. Or, the television screen is very large, or maybe it becomes virtual reality (VR). No matter what, it is an eerie experience. Without us taking charge, our child is left alone viewing and experiencing our old trauma as often as our *inner child* feels like it. As this occurs our mind is haunted by the echo of painful memories, unanswered calls for help,

broken relationship stories, sadness, traumatic proof of our *"I belong alone"* narrative.

Haunting is an important term here. Because it seems this little room is wired with an excellent sound system. If the TV is playing our trauma channel loudly, we will feel all our trauma feelings, we will likely get stuck —overwhelmed. We will not move on to the thinking section of our brains until we figure out how to turn down the volume, turn off the VR, or shut off the trauma channel completely. Once we have the capacity to resource our brain with problem-solving and self-soothing, we can better navigate our life's decisions and hopefully practice more *self-love* and then *love-energy, but when we are stuck in a state of overwhelm it is unlikely we are able to resource ourselves with love.*[1]

When we get stuck in our amygdala, we are stuck in the feeling center of our brain. When we act based on feelings, we will omit or limit our thinking, and we will almost always hit autopilot and default.

What are we to do with our *inner child* sitting in this little room? First, we make friends. Remember the photograph I asked you to find earlier? This is the child we are speaking of. If a different image comes to mind now that is also fine. Just notice. What is the picture you see of your inner, younger, child self?

With tenderness and gentleness, we approach this younger part of who we are, and we pay attention.

---

[1] Goleman, Daniel (1995). Emotional Intelligence: Why It Can Matter More Than IQ. Bantam Books.

We listen to their little voice. What do they say? We listen and we speak to our *inner child* with kindness, and I suggest, playfulness. We listen. We build a relationship with our inner child. We see how cute and loveable they are. They know we see how cute and loveable they are. We delight in them. They feel delighted in just as they are. Our loving mind knows our little child. *Self-love* ripples through us and through our younger self. We sit together in the *love-energy* of this renewed wholeness. We include this very important part of who we are in the wholeness of who we are.

The next time our *little child* flicks on our trauma channel, our rage channel, our self-harm channel, our manic happiness channel, our self-hate channel, or our flaw news report (there are many channels), we come to them and ask for the remote. As we sit together in *self-love*, they will trust us more and more.

We change the channel. We turn down the volume of our trauma. We remove the VR goggles. We take charge.

We learn we will love our own little child always. They are so damn loveable. Many of us will doubt this at the start. But, when we get slow and gentle, we make space to hear their little voice, to see their little presence, and to know their little identity.

Damn cute, your little one is.

Fall in love with your child.

Love and grieve the pain inflicted on a child you see as valuable,

A child that is easy for you to include in your own heart of love,

This child that is you.

Let your heart burst with how loveable you are.

All of you is loveable.

Your younger parts, your older parts.

All of your parts are loved and included.

Trauma impacts how we process our life. Remember, when we remain stuck in our trauma content the emotions associated with our trauma can cause us to be limited to move into the thinking center of our brain.[1] When we are stuck in our feelings without being informed by our thoughts, the trauma we have experienced, and re-experience, impacts our ability to process the world we are currently living in.

When you are stuck in your feelings, what does your trauma experience get you doing?

> Do you move more quickly through your life? Are you a "runner?" Do you run away from problems, or pain, or conflict? Are you a fighter? Are you mean? Suspicious? Cunning? Do you hit harder? Does your tongue get sharper? Do you put people in their place? Do you self-harm? Do you misuse yourself more? Do you punish yourself or others? Do you explode things? Do you make problems bigger than they are? Do you exaggerate? Do you freeze up? Do you minimize? Do you deny? Do you hide? Do you dissociate? Do you lose time? Do you lose people, or lose yourself to people?

---

[1] Van der Kolk, Bessel (2014). *The Body Keeps The Score: Brain, Mind, and Body in the Healing of Trauma.* Viking Press.

What does your trauma story get you doing?

> *Do you compound problems? Do you exaggerate how someone else has done you wrong? Do you placate and give in to others? Do you deny yourself an opinion? Do you blame yourself? Do you succumb to shame, blame, humiliation? What do you do?*

Self-love does not work when you love yourself in spite of yourself. *Self-love* is meant to pulse through your entire being, without spite. Loving your whole self, mess and all, will transform you. Meeting with your *inner child* in your little room called *the amygdala* will transform your *self-love* and shake up your questions about *love-energy*, then it will lead you to questions about supernatural love.

| Love is loving all the time, or it is not love.

Contemplative Question:

When will you set aside some time to enter into the little room inside your brain where your *inner child* is waiting for you to find them?

The next few chapters will center around the difficulty of forgiveness. There will be no pressure for you to figure out how to forgive people. I think you will be surprised to read what I have to say to you about forgiveness, amends, repair and reconciliation. These are important chapters. So, when you are ready, turn the page.

Love and Love's Energy

BEYOND FORGIVENESS

"Darkness cannot drive out darkness; only light can do that. Hate cannot drive out hate; only love can do that."
Martin Luther King Jr.[1]

There is a rush of pressure and responsibility that comes with the word forgiveness. One misconception many of us have been taught over the years is how the process of forgiveness is more a matter of responsibility. Whether we have been taught by someone else, or come to this assumption on our own, many of us see the forgiveness process as an action of us caring enough for someone else that we help them off the hook of their mistaken behavior.

Another common misconception is that "forgiveness helps me more than the other person." A lovely negative belief, which goes hand in hand with — "Forgive and forget." Both sound good, but they are not true reflections of forgiveness, moreover we will likely end up feeling terrible about ourselves for not being able to live up to either one. These beliefs are irrational, and risky when they become automatic thoughts. These ideas increase the risk of pride, increase the risk of a power differential, and heighten potential for martyrdom.

A third misconception about forgiveness is that it should mimic the court system and a judge. If the other person says the right words, if they emote enough

---

[1] Luther King, Jr., Martin (1986). *A Testament of Hope: The Essential Writings and Speeches.* HarperOne.

penance with their eyes, then our wooden mallet slams down, "Not guilty! You are no longer guilty in the eyes of my court!" Such a position of power. Power feels good when we are the ones holding the mallet. But we only need to have this experience once for us to see the unjust ways of "lady justice forgiveness." Many falsehoods have diluted our definition of forgiveness.

Eventually, something big will go down in our lives, and oversimplified forgiveness is not going to work. Forgetting the grievance will not happen. Then what?

> Some things in life stay left undone. When we believe we make ourselves responsible for all of the fractures in our relationships, we often view ourselves as the problem in our damaged relationships. We blame ourselves or we blame others. Then what is left undone becomes unsafe —we will likely worry this is yet another inner flaw.

We err by holding on to magical beliefs about forgiving and forgetting.

> Forgiveness which is in balance with amends, repair, and reconciliation is more of a process of refining. It is non-transactional. It is not a magic formula where we say the correct words and the grievance goes poof. Forgiveness is a relational experience.

It is worth noting: There is a place where an expression of apology and an expression of forgiveness may be uttered. It can feel really good when words are given to this process. But whatever words are given this process need not be transactional, and definitely need not be a formula.

Forgiveness done in haste or formula does not taste sweet.

It does not nourish.

It cannot be savored.

Forgiveness is not a quick fix.

It is layered.

It does not mean you spill your guts and leave "it" all behind.

Nor does forgiveness erase a "thing";

Our flaws forgiveness does not make to disappear.

Forgiveness is not magic.

Not a one and done,

Especially not with the big stuff, the mind-bending stuff.

True forgiveness teaches you to hear your inner voice, process your whole experience, and then speak about what you have endured. The hoped result is you will be all the more released from what you have done and what has been done to you.

It may be safe to go to the person who has done harm to you, but it may not be. Some people may have done unspeakable things to you. You are not required to go to them. Perhaps you have done grave damage to some people, and you may realize you will cause them even more damage by going to seek amends. You are valuable enough to have limits people who are unsafe for you, and people whom you are unsafe for. While this might be hard to wrap your mind around, some things are better left undone, left completely undone, or left undone for a time anyhow.

> Learning there are parts of our story that need to be left undone is helpful—scary and helpful. This is a new way of thinking. Forgiveness is a process of us evaluating our pain and asking: Do I process this

more with the other main characters in this story?

This is a crossroads of sorts, a chance to seek out a loving ear from an emotionally safe person. At times when we do not know what the story of forgiveness needs to look like, we can consult with others and give ourselves permission to talk about what troubles us about ourselves and other people. The more we do this the more we find out how to discuss our relationship woes without gossip and slander, and the better able we are to navigate forgiveness. Through emotionally safe consultation we can better navigate if forgiveness is possible.

You are not undeserving of love, as no one else is undeserving of love. Having boundaries with people who have caused you trauma and pain, being out of relationship with some people, does not make you less loveable, it also does not declare anyone else is less loveable. Being out of relationship feels like a defect, some additional flaw to feel bad about. But sometimes there is a place where you do not get reconciliation with other people. You will have these experiences, just as I will have these experiences, just as every other person will as well.

> Our experience of forgiveness is an experience of being heard by safe people, being loved by safe people, being seen and known by safe people, in the fullness of who we are.

Forgiveness is the act of hearing, seeing, and knowing someone as they express their erroneous behavior, and loving them as they are. Loving them as whole people. And it does not have to stop here. Making amends is going to someone we have wronged and authentically accounting for the error we have made to cause them harm. Amends requires sincere vulnerability within emotionally safe relationships. Making amends is active to repairing our relationships with others, and forgiveness is incomplete without it. Amends is us owning our contribution to someone else's pain. What is more, amends can give way to reconciliation. Reconciliation is a timeline of many meaningful, transformative moments of forgiveness and amends in the context of *love-energy*.

> Maybe reconciliation is always at the heart of love.

We may have experiences of forgiveness. We may have experiences of amends. Yet without reconciliation we still live with a polarized view of each other.

> Without reconciliation *we find crafty ways to win arguments. We become spectators of drama. We hold tightly to our opinions and judgments. We rely on the opinions of others. We hold no opinions at all. We puff up with power. We play the middle of the road. We become complacent. We hold grudges. We are spiteful. We forget, we change our minds, or compromise, or let someone else make a decision. We lose sight of other people's positive intentions.* With no reconciliation we miss out on corrective love.

Reconciliation is an expansive expression of forgiveness and amends within continued relationship. Reconciliation is one of the fullest expressions of *love-energy* because it is a timeline of many meaningful, transformative moments strung together. And, of course, reconciliation cannot happen without emotional safety.

> People can be offended when the word reconciliation is misused, and we should be.

There is no reconciliation without emotional safety. Reconciliation is not a checklist and it is never self-serving. Also, reconciliation requires informed consent, meaning that those who participate realize the nature of the reconciliation activity and the long-term commitment.

> May we be so blessed that we may endure and participate in reconciliation. Reconciliation done right is an expression of supernatural, transformative, corrective love — the fullest expression of *Love's Energy*.

Contemplative Questions:

What magical beliefs have you held about forgiveness? And how have these beliefs impacted you and our relationships?

How do you understand non-transactional forgiveness? What have you believed about reconciliation to this point?

What new insights do you have about forgiveness and reconciliation?

REPAIR

"If you look for truth, you may find comfort in the end; if you look for comfort you will not get either comfort or truth only soft soap and wishful thinking to begin, and in the end, despair."
C.S. Lewis[1]

We all have experienced a time when our need for love went unmet, and we have never forgotten. Even our beautiful close relationships can feel distant at times, maybe even broken. We can become angry and bitter at the people who are meant to show up for us. We can doubt they will ever actually show up for us, or we may even sabotage our relationships to make it impossible for them to show up for us.

In between forgiveness and repair we hope to find a way for our people to understand how desperately we need them, because we do need our people.

> In between forgiveness and repair, we protest distance in our relationships.

Whether you or I developed strategies of moving in or developed strategies of moving out of relationships, we are all doing this because we are deeply afraid of being alone, we are afraid to be outside of forgiveness, outside of repair. People who move in more do not care more about relationships and people who move out more do not care less.[2] Too often those who move out

---

[1] Lewis, C.S. (1952). Mere Christianity. Geoffrey Bles.

[2] Johnson, Sue (2008). Hold Me Tight: Seven Conversations for a Lifetime of Love. Little, Brown Spark.

get labeled as not caring for relationships, but they do. Also, people who bring the emotional heat do not care less about peace than the people who try to jump right into remedy and fixing. In-between forgiveness and repair our moving in and moving out of relationship often presents more intensely because we are more distressed.

In between forgiveness and repair there is space where we will be challenged to step further into processing what is broken between us and others, or not. In this space we need to have loving ears, loving eyes, and a loving mind to hear, see, and know our whole self; the more we know our whole self, the better we can navigate this in-between place with other people.

In between forgiveness and repair, we protest distance in our relationships.

Because somewhere inside of each one of us we all know

We are worthy of repair in our relationships.

Somewhere inside of us we all instinctively know

We are loved, loveable, and loving.

It is in our nature to love, and

It is in our nature to mourn the loss of any love that is left in disrepair.

Here is the best definition of repair I have come across:

> *"I am here, I know you need me, and we are going to work this out." —The Circle of Security*[1]

The entire process of repair takes vulnerability. We need to learn to self-reflect for us to be able to move out of our faulty beliefs about there being correct

---

[1] Hoffman, Kent, Copper, Glen, Powell, Bert (2017). *Raising a Secure Child How Circle of Security Parenting Can Help You Nurture Your Child's Attachment, Emotional Resilience, and Freedom to Explore.* Guilford Press.

words or behaviors that will "fix" things. There is no magic pill for repair. No quick fix. No one size fits all phrase. Repair becomes possible as we become noticers.

We notice ourselves.

We notice others.

We wonder about how to be present,

How to be available and helpful,

To meet someone else in their place of need.

What value does it hold to overcomplicate this process? When did we become so strenuous about repair? Why do we believe there is merit in analyzing and professing who is more damaging in relationships and who needs to be sorrier about their terrible behavior?

| Repair is not a drama production.

When we get into these loops of analyzing and comparing wounds, we almost always forget the simple answer is always love.

> Repair is about the reciprocal experience of hearing with loving ears, seeing with loving eyes, and knowing with a loving mind. The vice versa of giving and receiving the energy of love.

This does not mean repair is about making things equal or balanced. In repair, we experience being loveable together. We have more certainty we are loved. We have more proof we are loving. We live in such a way that other people can believe the same is true for them.

The words "I am sorry" may never be spoken. The word "forgive" may never be used in this process. A well worded amends may not happen. We may not even quite know what words of repair we piece together.

Repair is reciprocal and non-transactional love; repair is a product of *love-energy*. With more repair we trust more in our own value. We learn to believe in the value of others even more. We trust in our own lovability. We see the lovableness in others. We stop rejecting the flawed parts of ourselves. We stop rejecting the flaws of others. We accept ourselves as whole people. We accept others as whole people. We see ourselves as capable of calming down our shame about our wrong behavior. We find we are willing to admit our mistakes. This is where repair happens.

> Where do we begin the repair process with others? *Sitting in the same room, giving someone space when they ask for it, revisiting painful content and talking it through, admitting error.* "I didn't get that right, did I?" "I can see your point of view." "I am angry, you are right." "I didn't make time." "I have time now and I want to hear you through." *Seeing someone's emotion and guessing which one you see, being okay with being in the wrong, risking rejection, risking our own flaws being seen, dropping our defaults, being messy, these are ways that lead to repair.* "I am okay if things get a little messy right now while we try to figure this out."

Loving ourselves and accepting ourselves as we are, offering love to someone else without an agenda, being vulnerable with our own self, then being vulnerable with another, opens the door to authentic amends and connection.

"I am here, I know you need me, and we are going to work this out," says the Circle of Security.[1]

Write it down. Meditate on it. Get this statement into your heart.

Contemplative Question:

What is in between forgiveness and repair for you?

Take some time to consider examples in your life when you have experienced repair. How do you notice these times?

What are some ways you hear others with loving ears?

Ways you see others with loving eyes?

Ways you know others with a loving mind?

In times of disrepair how do you hear yourself with loving ears, see yourself with loving eyes and know yourself with a loving mind?

---

[1] Hoffman, Kent, Copper, Glen, Powell, Bert (2017). *Raising a Secure Child How Circle of Security Parenting Can Help You Nurture Your Child's Attachment, Emotional Resilience, and Freedom to Explore.* Guilford Press.

Love and Love's Energy

A CONTEMPLATION FOR RECONCILIATION

At the heart of reconciliation is always love, or it is not.

Reconciliation happens within relationships where the past is acknowledged,

Where there is a shared agreement for hope and a future,

Or it is not.

Reconciliation is not bound to a timeline because

It has no predicted sequence,

It does not happen all at once;

It is deeply personal, and always unique,

Always loving, and

It is always to be held with gentleness and curiosity.

It is alive,

It needs breath,

It needs be nurtured.

It heals. It helps. It hopes.

Reconciliation restores what we believed to be lost;

It prophesies we all belong.

It honors everyone's value for no other reason than

The reason that every one exists.

"Every one exists and everyone belongs!"

Reconciliation restores our belief in love.

Reconciliation draws us further and further into the mystery of love.

It leads us to question the meaning of life and

The vastness of love-energy;

It asks us to question the influence Love's Energy has over our ever existence.

By it we are transformed, changed forever.

We awaken to a new way of being with each step we take

Toward

New life,

New love,

New hope,

Renewed awe.

Reconciliation knows that the mystery of relationships need continual

Revisiting,

Revising, and

Refreshing.

Reconciliation is

Hearing with loving ears, seeing with loving eyes, and knowing with a loving mind;

Without expiration.

Reconciliation beckons us to know we are

Loved, loveable, and loving. Inasmuch as

It is a revelation that every one of us is loved, loveable and loving;

That every one is reconciled to the same heart of love as everyone else.

Reconciliation convinces us we are all included.

With no agenda.

With no urgency.

No greatness or folly, No gender or race,

No trauma,

No hate,

Not one thing is beyond reconciliation.

Each one of us is deserving

To be reconciled to ourselves, to each other, to humanity, and

To Creator God.

Give reconciliation time.

Give it emotionally safe space to age

With one's self,

With each other,

With our Creator,

Until there is no other.

Reconciliation is the heartbeat of the Creator resounding through

The very one of us, and the every one of us.

Love and Love's Energy

LOVE'S ENERGY

May we find Love's Energy as it is meant for us.
This love that has never been lost to us,
Is found in us,
And further integrated.

And now we have arrived at our final section. We have explored *love-energy* and *self-love*. We have considered proof of our loved, loveable and loving nature. We have looked at theory and considered story as well as metaphors and therapeutic tools. And here we have arrived to turn our attention to supernatural love. What is *Love's Energy*? Let's find out!

Love and Love's Energy

FALLING INTO LOVE

"Love and do what you will."
St. Augustine[1]

At one point in my personal story, I was being deeply challenged by a mentor on my beliefs and experience of my own attachment style and how I present my life —my defaults. As he was teaching and I was reflecting, I began to experience something new. I was having a new experience of *"the need to get under the surface."* I heard a voice within myself say, *"You can fall in, give yourself permission."*

Will you fall into who you are on the inside?

Will you make friends with your fear about who you are?

It is frightening to fall into your inner chasm. It seems an abyss at the start. You will feel fear.

Will you fall into your whole self?

This is the beginning of discovering

Love's Energy.

Will you fall into love?

What may come with this *falling into love*?

Tears, honesty, admitting unmet longings, seeing our flaws, seeing our faults, seeing our need for people, being accountable, changing behaviors, quitting behaviors, being confused, righteous anger,

---

[1] Saint Augustine (2014). *The Four Books of St. Augustine on Christian Doctrine.* IndoEuropeanPublishing.com.

grieving, giving up control, messy feelings, mistakes, more mistakes, shame, sorrow, guilt, feeling feelings, making amends, self-doubt, boundaries, changed relationships, changed behaviors, loss of relationships, new relationships, and many, many questions. But also, more self-knowledge, more self-love, better relationships with others, laughter, joy, mystery, inspiration, healing, self-acceptance, emotional awareness and regulation, less shame, less fear, more peace, more hope, more meaning and purpose. Eventually landing in the knowledge we are loved, loveable, loving, and included.

When we give ourselves permission to fall into our whole self, we learn to tenderly observe the root of our pain and the meaning of why we do what we do. We can become abundantly aware of the energy of loving ourselves, and the energy of loving the people around us. We discover *love-energy* is a mirror of *Love's Energy*. We become more curious about *Love's Energy*— the great mass of love we are all connected to? We fall more in love with who we are and discover that our whole self is vibrant with unique perfectly-imperfect details. We become more and more reconciled with ourselves, more and more reconciled with love, more reconciled with others, more curious.

We experience more and more love with other people, then even more reconciliation with ourselves and others. We see love all around us—the vibrance of *Love's Energy* pulses through us and through each person we meet.

Love is what we are born into.

Love is what we are born for.

We are created by love to be loved, loveable and loving.

There is freedom in Love's Energy.

What was once heavy becomes manageable.

What we once despised in ourselves we now love.

What was once shameful and to be hidden becomes loveable.

Where we used to need to shield ourselves from the world's view,

We find ourselves loving our fellow person.

We find a sense of belonging in our own self because of the love we are participating in.

We fall in, and

We fall in love with who we are.

We lose the urgency to design our own life.

This self-discover is a love discovery, a falling in love with love. And it does not have to stop for us.

We fall in love with love.

Our heart knows something new:

There is more love to know.

Love's Energy compels us.

It comforts us.

It beckons us to know the vast expanse of all of the energy of love.

We live in epiphany.

We make room for other people;

We hope for relationships.

We make room to marvel at the world around us;

We question the mystery of love anew.

We have more space for new questions about love and Love's origin.

Start by trying to do *self-love*, and love will bring you to the place where you ask someone else to join you.

And then consider, if you will, just how vast is *Love's Energy?*

"You can fall in, give yourself permission."

Love is powerful. It will do its *love-energy* thing. After all, s*elf-love* and *love-energy* belong to supernatural love — *Love's Energy.*

The pace you go, the help you afford yourself, the help afforded to you, the different ways you build self-contemplation, when and where you have new experiences of relationships, how you sense into love, how you give love, how you do discovery of... or rediscovery of God, is your unique story, your mystery.

The supernatural energy of love will be found by you because it has never been lost to you.

Love's Energy has never been lost to you.

Knowing *Love's Energy* is knowing the heartbeat of love. Our supernatural *"magical hour"* is realizing the heartbeat of love belongs to God.

Contemplative Questions:

Will you fall into love?

Will you give yourself permission?

It will take courage to consider Love's design.

A NEW VIEW OF LOVE

"We cannot give ourselves to God if we do not belong to ourselves. And we do not belong to ourselves if we belong to our own ego."
Thomas Merton[1]

It is okay if the God piece is still problematic. What I will say about God is that God has thick skin. You don't have to believe *Love's Energy* belongs to God. For some of you, it is healthy to not believe this at this point in your love recovery. Because God has thick skin, it may serve you much more to vent all of the ugly feelings you have about a god who has let your life be fractured by pain and fear.

| Start where you start.

When I first learned to trust the humanistic experience, the science and the theory of it all, I became curious to discover the vast expression of love. This is where I found God. I did not mean to, I had made peace with who I thought God was, and I had submitted to my beliefs in a God who was not necessarily going to include me. I had made peace with my lonely inner self. I had accepted I was "sitting outside the gates," I had given up on having assurance that I was truly accepted by God, just the way I was.

---

[1] Merton, Thomas (1950). Seasons of Celebration: Meditations on the Cycle of Liturgical Feasts. Farrar, Strays and Giroux, LLC.

But attachment science taught me about love. Love worked on me and my inner fears and flaws, and my *heartlessness*. My view of love shifted. And as Love loved me, my old view of God didn't fit anymore. None of my views fit anymore. I discovered love is more than love, it is *self-love, love-energy* and at its source it is *Love's Energy*. Because at the source of love is always God.

I did get lost and angry. I had moments where I raged against God. God has thick skin, remember. I have sworn at God. I have let myself wonder if God exists. I have discovered that all of me —my flaws, fear, my *heartlessness* and my defaults— is touched by *Love's Energy*. It took as long as it took for me to let Love love me. To let Love reveal to me my *pure-of-heartness*.

Whatever we have been taught to believe about the risks of being banished from God's heart, we need to find courage to challenge these. We are included, which may seem foreign. But we are included in love. Anything that tells us *you are not* is a lie. Being told we must live in such a way that we rid ourselves of all flaws is a lie, and unloving. We are whole people, and we are wholly loved by God.

God loves us as whole people before we love ourselves as whole people. *Love's Energy* embraces all of who we are and each one of us just as we are. We are dappled, and damaged, unique, and loved, and loveable and loving because we are included. T h i s is *Love's Energy;* It echoes God's heartbeat.

We all have blind spots. The more we go down this path, the more we get to discover and rediscover the parts of ourselves that are actually causing us pain and disconnection. It has taken time to get to this place. We go at our own pace. We offer ourselves gentleness. We encourage others to go at their own pace. We are mindful that everyone else is making their own discovery, or non-discovery.

Love is already here.

There is no need to convince anyone of a love we are already included in.

We all belong to love.

Contemplative Questions:

What is your old view of love?

What is your view of God old and new?

How are your views of love changing?

How are your views of God changing?

What are your thoughts about *Love's Energy?*

Love's Energy oozes our being loved, loveable and loving.

Love and Love's Energy

YOU ARE LOVED, LOVEABLE, & LOVING

"I will greet this day with love in my heart.

Henceforth will I love all humankind. From this moment all hate is let from my veins for I have not time to hate, only time to love. From this moment I take the first step required to become a man among men... If I have no other qualities, I can succeed with love alone. Without it I will fail though I possess all the knowledge and skills of the world."
Og Mandino[1]

Recently I sat with a client who has worked hard in their attachment landscape. We were doing family therapy, and in this session, this parent did some beautiful parent things. I could feel love transforming all the energy in the entire room. Out of my deep respect and admiration, I said to this parent, *"You know you are so loved. You are so loveable. And you are so loving."* To which they replied, "That is mind bending for me." Their lip quivered, "That one will take some time for me to know what to do with."

You are loved. The original source of our being loved is God's heart. Can you learn to hear the heartbeat of *Love's Energy?* Listening to the heartbeat of God, like a newborn infant, we are reminded of the place we have always belonged —like parent and child coregulating the hour after birth, we experience *Love's*

---

[1] Mandino, Og (1983). *The Greatest Salesman in the World.* Bantam; Reissue edition.

Energy as profoundly as a *magical* heart-to-heart hug. We catch the beat.

> *Love's Energy knows us.*
>
> *Love's Energy sees us.*
>
> *Love's Energy hears us.*
>
> *Love's Energy is supernatural, and it is the truest expression of love.*
>
> *Love's Energy is always abundant love— love to be explored.*

As we explore love we find peace to know we are included in the same heart of love as everyone else. As we begin to trust we are included in love, of course we can begin to trust we are loved.

> *Love's Energy is the pulse of God's heart.*
>
> *The same heart of love we are all included in.*

The natural design of our human survival is bent toward nurture because our human nature is not enough. We are wired for relationship, and because we have experience of damaged love it is natural to wonder about God's loving nature. It is okay to wonder if God's love is damaged or damaging, but it is not. God's love is loving, or it is not.

We learn about love, and we have to question our old views of God. Does a God who holds fire bolts in his hands and habitually ignores masses of people hold us all in the same heart of love? From an attachment point of view, this makes no sense. Consider this purely from the position of parenting— try to parent with lightning bolts and "*magical hours*" simultaneously and see how you feel as a parent, furthermore, see the results in your child. This type of parenting will confuse a child's attachment, we may even use the term disorganized attachment.[1] Do we believe in a God whose deity works to disorganize our experience of secure base and safe haven with our Creator? Why?

It is utterly unnatural, largely impossible, for us to be at peace when we ascribe violence to Love's Energy. God's love is consistently loving.

You are loved by God.

You are known by God.

You are seen by God, and you are heard by God. It is hard enough to believe in our human experience of love. It is okay to distrust *Love's Energy*. For most of us, our understanding of God's love is confusing. It is too hard to think about. Most of us stop ourselves. But God's love is worth wrestling through. It is one of, if not, the most important philosophies to wonder on: God's inclusive love.

You are loveable. Your version of *"I belong alone,"* will have you wondering if maybe you don't deserve as much love as the person sitting beside you. But you do. And I do. Everyone does.

The more experiences we have of love, the better we become at evaluating which people are our people— the people who love us. Having human experiences of being loveable helps us to be curious about God. *Is God loving?* (No need to answer, we are wondering). When we do not trust we are loveable by human standards, the less we risk considering if God finds us loveable.

> Being heard with loving ears, being seen with loving eyes, and being known by the loving mind of another person is corrective— it is an epiphany

---

[1] Bowlby, John. (1988). A Secure Base: Parent-Child Attachment and Healthy Human Development. Basic Books.

of love-energy. This is love. This is the fullest expression of us being loved solely for the sake of knowing we are lovable. Our human love is a powerful reminder that Love's Energy is always knowing, always seeing, and always hearing us with love. Trusting in a love like this is hard for most of us. I keep a personal record of my wrongdoings; I think most people do. At least, I hear many people speak about doing something similar. I am able to recount the worst of my cringe-worthy mistakes and set up the TV in my mind's eye to watch hours of programming. All on my own, I provide myself with detailed graphics of my incompetence—proof of how unlovable I am.

I see a mass theme with people, me included, who worry other people will believe the worst about us. We cannot rewind time, we can't go back and erase the past, so we worry. What we have gotten wrong is etched in our stories. We have no choice when it comes to past mistakes, and there are more mistakes to come. But we are whole people, past mistakes and all. You are loveable. I am loveable. People are loveable. No matter what.

> The beautiful design of love is how love does not only occur in the good times. Love also occurs in the bad times, times when we have to dig deep and meet ourselves and others in our messy human moments.

You are loving. There is proof of this as you venture to look for it. Don't let your record of your own wrongdoings distract you from the times you are present for other people. Don't let your record of wrongs get in the way of trusting you have a loving nature, of feeling your ability to be a catalyst for *love-*

energy, allowing *self-love* to dance through you, to learn more about your capacity to get it wrong and love yourself and others through your blunders.

Equally as important, don't let your record of wrongs get in the way of building capacity to wonder about *Love's Energy*. Your whole self, your blunders and your brilliance, all belong because of *Love's Energy*.

You are designed to hear other people with loving ears, to see other people with loving eyes, to know other people with your loving mind, when you can and as you can. You have gotten this right at times and gotten this wrong at other times. The times you err do not erase your loving nature, as you now know you do not erase any part of you. Be cognizant of your love experiences. Be a noticer. Be a ponderer of love and love-energy.

Your love.

Other's love.

Supernatural love.

Unfathomable love.

Fathomable love. Mysterious love. Understood love.

Our loved, loveable, loving nature is how we participate in Love's Energy.

Participating in Love's Energy is our fullest expression and experience of love.

Contemplative Questions:

What does it mean for you to believe you are loved?

For you to believe you are loveable?

For you to believe you are loving?

What do you believe about *Love's Energy?*

You and I, and everyone else are so very included in the same heart of love as everyone else. It is a beautiful truth to know, and a marvel for us to continue to understand. So, shall we?

BEING INCLUDED IN LOVE'S HEART

*"When you love you should not say, 'God is in my heart',
but rather, 'I am in the heart of God'."*
Kahlil Gibran[1]

None of us are better than any other. We are all included. We have always been included. We err when we think we need to design a presence in this world that will allow us to fit in. We are whole people who belong.

Brené Brown has shared how her research has proven that the opposite of fitting in is belonging.[2] Our defaults are our attempt to fit in. However, love is proof of us always belonging. To belong is very different than to fit in.

We are included in the same heart of love as everyone else. We always have been. We always will be included in *Love's heart*. Believing in a love like this has been a work in progress in each of our lives to this point. It will continue to be a work in progress for each of us from this point forward. The thing about love is we experience and discover love at our own pace. No Rush. Love will do what it needs to do.

| Love keeps pace with our pace.

---

[1] Gibran, Kahlil (1923). *The Prophet*. Alfred A. Knopf.

[2] Brown, Brené (2021). *Atlas of the Heart: Mapping Meaningful Connection and the Language of Human Experience*. Random House.

I need not convince you of what love is. Discussing love gets you thinking about love, noticing the love around you, your experience and expression of love, and eventually wondering about *Love's Energy*.

> *We start talking about love.*
>
> *We start exploring love.*
>
> *Love does the rest.*
>
> *Because Love's Energy is wondrous.*
>
> *And, when it comes to supernatural love, wonder away.*

We belong in the same heart of love as everyone else without having to figure out the method to fit.

> *We are included before we ask,*
>
> *Even before we know we need to ask.*
>
> *We belong regardless of who we are.*
>
> *Each other person belongs regardless of who they are.*
>
> *We are all whole people, and we are included.*
>
> *Love's Energy includes us.*

We are discovering all the more that we are loved, loveable, and loving. As we discover this, we naturally join with others in light of these truths. As others make these same discoveries, they will join us too. We are included in the same heart of love and love unfolds as it will because love does unfold.

Consider using the following affirmation for your own love discovery. If you see this affirmation is helpful you can copy it and place it somewhere where you will remember to repeat and reflect. Positive love affirmations are worth reflecting on, even committing to memory:

Love's Energy accepts my whole self. *Love's Energy* accepts the whole self of the person sitting next to me as well. I am included in God's heart. I belong. I belong and I don't have to work hard to fit in. I am loved no matter how I have screwed things up in my past or how I may screw things up in my tomorrow. I am loved no matter how powerfully I believe I am destined to be alone. Because I am not destined to be alone. Love includes me.

We live in love.

We hear love's heartbeat.

We see Love's Energy, and we know we are known by love. This Energy is mystery,

It is adventure, It is comfort, This Love is peace of soul. This Love is life.

Catching the heartbeat of love we are drawn more fully into Love's Energy. Discovering we are included in God's loving heart, no matter what. This changes everything.

This is an absolute truth: we are included.

Will we believe?

Will we adventure with love?

Love encourages us to take risks and to explore,

And to always come back to the heart of love.

We take aim at life and love supports us.

It helps us make sense of ourselves in light of love.

It casts light into the dark places of our own identity

As it casts light into the dark places of the world around us. Love's Energy:

God's loving energy.

Our ultimate experience of "I belong alone" is thinking we are separated from a love that is steady to assure we belong. We are always included in *Love's Energy*.

Contemplative Question:

What picture do you paint in your mind's eye of the heart of love?

Writing about God's love like I am will sound very different people. I am writing about a God who I believe is loving, and whom I believe designed us with not only human nature but human need for nurturing. A God who designed us. I am upholding that there is clear scientific proof of how loving relationships benefit our evolutionary survival— *love-energy*. I am unsure how else to understand God's love for humanity but by this discovery of what loving relationships are intended to be. Exploring attachment theory has caused me to wonder at the marvel of what love is, and how love ultimately is designed.

> God is loving, and we are afforded the ability to discover just how loving God is.

GOD'S LOVE IS LOVING

"It would be a great mistake to turn the interior life into a psychological experiment and make our prayer the object of psychoanalysis."
Thomas Merton[1]

Love is loving.

May we be present as we consider the loving nature of Love's Energy.

Like Merton's comment, let us not psychoanalyze our interior life. Let us practice presence. Like being lost in the movement of dance, or singing a good song, or falling into a dream as we drift to sleep. If we turn our brain on too intensely, we pull ourselves out of the energy of the moment. Let's hold space for the loving energy of love.

> Loving moments are often small but they make big shifts.

I will sit with people for hours, then all of a sudden, the energy around this person shifts, literally in the blink of an eye. After many conversations where I participate in holding space for someone, where they are heard, seen, and known, all of a sudden something shifts. I have little idea which one conversation is going to be the one where a client will sink more into their experience of *love-energy*, but I trust the energy of love, I need to do little but to hold space for love to be loving.

---

[1] Merton, Thomas (2004). *The Inner Experience: Notes on Contemplation.* HarperOne; Reprint edition.

I often think of nuts and bolts, though I rarely remember which is which. (I did look it up again right now.) I like to think of how a loose nut does not need to be turned a great deal for it to be secured on the bolt. Tightening a nut takes purposeful movement as well as an awareness that without attention the loose nut will become problematic. Turning the nut to tighten it on the bolt secures the nut without us considering how many twists of the wrench, or how many rotations the nut needed. This is much like how *love-energy* surrounds people. We make a slight adjustment by talking about a seemingly small thing, but the twist of the small content adjusts the balance of the whole person. As the nut and bolt belong together, so too do people and love.

It is good to purposefully consider moments where we are heard, seen, and known. We have a view of the world around us rooted in our own experiences. As our mind is set on love, how we view the world around us changes.

We notice the parent and child laughing in the park, the couple splashing each other at the beach. We savor our colleague joking with us and the twinkle in their eye as they share a quip for our benefit. We notice those who hold hands as they walk, the way a caregiver pats a child's head, the dad high-fiving their teen after a big game, the teenagers glued together giggling, the young couple on a date at a steak restaurant, the grocery clerk laughing with a regular customer, the seniors having a dance in the senior home. We see the energy of love all around us, and it looks loving. The fact that the loving nature of love is universal and collective draws us further into *Love's Energy*.

Love has always looked loving, but our view of love is shifting for the better. It is safer to see the good intention behind the moments we catch between people. Our own love experiences can now inspire us to seek more opportunities to offer *love-energy*. The more *love-energy* we experience with other people the more we discover that *love-energy* is our participation in *Love's Energy*. We increasingly feel a part of the universality of it all.

Self-love.

Love-energy.

Love's Energy.

They ebb and flow and belong together.

When we think too hard about the dad who high-fives their teen after the big game, it is possible we will naturally drop into cynicism. We need not psychoanalyze. We are now noticers of these moments. Loving moments, we collect and store in our mind. Knowing all others have capacity to observe and collect similar moments. We collect these moments as we see them, not analyzing what grave flaws everyone else has. The love inside of us feels connected to the *love-energy* in the moment we witness, and the larger mass of *Love's Energy* that we all belong to. This takes practice and intention. Again, we start where we start with this love process. Love is always around us, and in us. We are designed to see the world with loving eyes. To be noticers of the loving nature of love. Seeing the world this way attunes our hearing and softens our mind, Love flows through us and around us.

As we look around at other people experiencing these love moments, we don't have to do much more other than stop ourselves from dissecting what we see. Dissecting people's actions is one way we default, to theorize about the inevitable root flaw in others. We see people living and breathing their moment of miracle, their moment of loving, and we catch the beat. They are included in the same heart of love as we are.

We catch the beat of

Loving love.

We are experiencers of love.

We are noticers of love.

We are participants in this way.

What is curious is the moments we expect to be big core memories may not be. This is why we can observe small moments between strangers and see *love-energy*. We call them flashbulb memories. Flashbulb memories can be good or bad, but they are memories that carry such profound impact we recall them with vivid detail— the location, the clothes we were wearing, song on the radio, smell in the air, sometimes even the exact date.[1] These are the memories that get stored in our internal television, in the little room in our brain called the amygdala.

We have already discussed our trauma channel, but we also have a love channel. It is possible to store stories and images of *love-energy,* it is possible for us to learn to turn this channel on and enjoy the content. We may even start to mindfully begin to choose which love stories we download to our love channel.

Witnessing the love all around us, we connect with the experiences we have had of love throughout our own lives. We connect with our body and how the energy of love feels inside of us. We already know love is loving, and we want to dwell and expand this wisdom.

[1] Brown, Roger, Kulik, James (1977). Flashbulb Memories. Cognition 5 (1); 73-99.

No matter how love has been injured in our personal story, we can do this. When we can, as we can.

> We see love. We feel love. We know love is loving.

Love-energy between people is a beautiful inspiration for us. As love unfolds all around us, we see and savor it, and our bodies become better at savoring how love feels inside of us. We wonder more about how God's love is loving. Experiencing *self-love* helps us to wonder about this too. We love ourselves, we love other people, and we wonder more about the vastness of God's love.

> We experience these big and little love moments. We feel the loving force of them no matter their size. Our bodies naturally participate in love. We discover love really does have design in us. Love truly is where we all belong. *Love's heart —Love's Energy.*

It is an existential shift, like being born. We are born into love. Renewing our view of love changes everything for us. Love touches all the parts of who we are and still loves us. We are whole people. We need only be present in our experiences of *love-energy* and *self-love*, and let love include us in *Love's Energy*, the same heart of love we all belong to.

Like all existential shifts, love lends itself to moments of corrective epiphanies. Where the inclusiveness of love wraps itself around us.

God's love and our love mingle. We contemplate this new epiphany —we are loved and created for love. We join in. We reciprocate. We notice God's love for the world around us. We notice God's love for us. We see our love for ourselves, for others and for God is transformative.

Contemplative Questions:

How does it feel to observe strangers and see the energy of their relationship in a single moment?

How do you notice these moments in your body?

How will you cultivate your practice of noticing *love-energy*?

What does *love-energy* teach you about *Love's Energy*? I am sure you have many good questions stirring inside of you, I hope you are keeping track of these, they are worth writing down. Questioning love is as important as questioning God, and both are very welcome as emotionally safe conversations about love and a loving God occur.

One big problem many people have is that we have been made to believe we should fear God. Fearing a loving God should be confusing, we should realize such a view is impossible to reconcile, at least from an attachment perspective. I will do my best to lay a foundation for how correction has a place in love, even where punishment does not.

CAN GOD BE LOVING AND CORRECTING?

"Ruptures are inevitable, repair is optional."
The Circle of Security[1]

When we think of God's love, it is natural to compare God's love to the love of a parent or caregiver. Human love is a mirror of God's love.

> As a caregiver hears their child with loving ears, this child can learn to *loving*ly hear themselves.

> As a caregiver sees their child with loving eyes, this child can be in the fullness of who they are, messy flaws and all, and this child can better learn to see they are beautiful *lovable* as a whole person.

> As a caregiver knows their child with a loving mind, this child is better able to confront their fear of being alone —this child has more assurance they are *loved*.

> This child can choose to exist in the fullness of who they are, as often as possible.

Children make mistakes and parents need to correct them. The goal is to correct them in love. It is hard to

---

[1] Hoffman, Kent, Copper, Glen, Powell, Bert (2017). *Raising a Secure Child How Circle of Security Parenting Can Help You Nurture Your Child's Attachment, Emotional Resilience, and Freedom to Explore.* Guilford Press.

believe, but it is possible for correction to always happen within love.

What does attachment theory teach us about the balance between love and correction? Bowlby calls this balance *"safe haven"* and *"secure base."*[1] A parent offers a *"secure base"* where kids jump off of the relationship and out into the world, then they jump back and land into a welcoming *"safe haven"* where they experience their parent's love as comforting and accepting and also as correcting and accepting. Imagine the benefits this offers a child? Imagine the long-term positive effect on adults who have been children in such experiences? And here is a greater truth to wonder on *"safe haven"* and *"secure base"* are a mirror of God's love and correction.

Decades ago, Bowlby also introduced us to the caregiver concept of *"stronger, wiser, other."*[2] The Circle of Security folks elaborate to define the caregiving position as *"bigger, stronger, wiser and kind."*[3] Both word groupings are utterly inspired, representing how we big people can influence little people's lives well. Another greater truth to wonder on, all of this good parenting intention is a reflection of God's loving intention.

> Loving correction is a core experience. Loving correction is helpful and not harmful. It is not based on power when it is *bigger, stronger, wiser and kind*. It is not rash. It comes from a place of experience and understanding. It is tuned in to

---

[1] Bowlby, John. (1988). *A Secure Base: Parent-Child Attachment and Healthy Human Development.* Basic Books.

[2] Bowlby, John. (1988). *A Secure Base: Parent-Child Attachment and Healthy Human Development.* Basic Books.

[3] Hoffman, Kent, Copper, Glen, Powell, Bert (2017). *Raising a Secure Child How Circle of Security Parenting Can Help You Nurture Your Child's Attachment, Emotional Resilience, and Freedom to Explore.* Guilford Press.

the emotion of the one being corrected. It is
balanced by emotional safety. It is inspired and
inspiring. It is within the continuum of
reconciliation. Love based correction provides
space for bother *"safe haven"* and *"secure base."*

God only offers emotionally safe correction. God's correction is rooted in love. It is strong and wise and kind. God's design is that no one will be corrected outside of love. Correction that occurs outside of love, as defined by attachment theory, is not loving, and therefore not God's design, because attachment theory is God's design for nurture in relationships. God's design is for no one to be corrected outside of God's love.

Correction within love is always possible. Correction never needs violence. Correction never needs punishment. Violence or punishment is never prerequisite for transformation to occur.

Love is always transformative. If violence or punishment occurs, love can cover even these mistakes. *Love's Energy* always holds space for us to find repair for the mistakes we make.

Unloving corrections are downloaded in our brain onto our trauma channel. These stories of what is unloving in our life naturally makes us doubt love. When we are taught correction and love are separate, we believe a lie. Being taught unloving correction is acceptable is a lie. Being taught unloving correction is within God's love is also a lie. And as with all traumatic lies, it is downloaded the same.

Correction apart from love is not God's design. Correction apart from love disorganizes all of our relationships including our relationship with God. This lie needs undoing and needs to be replaced with the truth.

> Love is loving. God's correction is loving. Correction outside of love is not from God. God's correction is stronger, wiser and always including.

Contemplative Questions:

What have you believed about God's correction?

How have you believed God uses love and correction separately?

What does it mean that correction is meant to coincide with love? Do you trust God's correction is always loving?

As we learn to trust that God's love is both safe and correcting, we have space to wonder about just how far-reaching God's love is. We can have more hope for how completely we are included in God's love. Because if I am included, and you are included, then everyone else is too. This is amazing to believe and worth expanding on.

INDISCRIMINATE LOVE

"Love has no other desire but to fulfil itself."
Kahlil Gibran[1]

A couple of winters ago, as the snow piled up in Alberta, I hopped on a zoom call with David Hayward, also known as the Naked Pastor.[2] David is an amazing soul and an important voice for us messy people. As I spoke with David, I asked him what he thought about love, and he had brilliant things to offer. Two words stuck with me the most: *"Indiscriminate Love."*

When David said this, it was a beautiful moment for me. I felt such a well of emotion inside. I had a *"that's it"* moment:

What we are really longing for is to be heard, seen, and known in the grips of indiscriminate love. To be, just be, as we are, and still experience love. To be messy and flawed and loved. To not have to rely on our defaults. To experience moments of assurance, regardless of what we have done, where we hear the heartbeat of love, and we feel love pulse in us. To actually hear the voice of *Love's Energy* say: *"You are always included in indiscriminate love."*

---

[1] Gibran, Kahlil (1923). *The Prophet*. Alfred A. Knopf.
[2] nakedpastor.com.

This fits well with all we are leaning into about love. Indiscriminate love is the type of love babies are born to experience. This is the type of *love-energy* we experience in corrective epiphanies. This type of love is *Love's Energy*. Indiscriminate love is the heartbeat we are all trying to catch.

| *Love's Energy* is indiscriminate.

Indiscriminate love really is our inheritance. I worry about using the word inheritance because it has some old religious use and generational abuse to it. But when we think about the intention of inheritance, it does really fit.

Love's Energy is already ours.

It is available to us.

We are included in it's will. It does not belong more to anyone else,

It is an inheritance for all. Even if we set ourselves independent from this inheritance, We are still written into the heart of indiscriminate love. Yet, we always still have a choice to participate.

This love does not discriminate, and it does not require us to consent to it.

Here me out: What might happen when we trust we are heirs of *Love's Energy*? Heirs of the energy that is God's fullest supernatural expression of enduring. If we, in turn, bestow an inheritance of love onto others? What if we do not discriminate who we love? What if we place no conditions on the love we offer? If we learn to receive and give love trusting we all are heirs of indiscriminate love, could we know love more fully? Could we be transformed in this way?

> Love is not something we are waiting for, it is a living, breathing, available, present, abundant, nondiscriminatory inheritance. That's a lot of love!

We can all get a little love drunk, which is great at times. But it is hard to be human and trust our own ability to offer this kind of love to others, especially when we doubt we deserve it ourselves. Learning to trust we are included takes time. Love does not discriminate against you or anyone else. This takes time to trust, so take all the time you need; this is your love discovery.

> You are included and so am I. You are an heir to indiscriminate love and so am I.

We have been born to be included and we are meant to participate in relationships free of discrimination. We are loved, loveable, and loving— always. Where human relationships falter, we are still included in *Love's Energy*, which is the source of all nondiscrimination. This love does not falter because *Love's Energy* is the source of all non-violence.

Don't allow your trauma to take responsibility for your life. Don't allow your flaws to be in charge of you or your love. Take off your old view and let love inform the goodness of your lookout. Let love inspire you to know your value as a whole person. This is not an easy suggestion. We need only start somewhere, when we can, as we can. Let love do the rest.

Will you learn to honor your goodness in moments when you are:

gentle, calm, peaceful, friendly, joyful, funny, lighthearted, smart, thoughtful, quiet, wise, helpful, confident, inspired, still, when you are in blessing, when you are in love, when you are in beauty?

It is hard to trust our inner beauty. Unbelievably hard to trust our innate goodness. But these moments are valuable parts of our whole self. These moments resound with indiscriminate love.

Moments of presence.

Pure-of-heart moments.

Indiscriminate love moments.

Contemplative Questions:

What might it mean to adopt indiscriminate *self-love*?

To offer indiscriminate *love-energy* for others?

What are your beliefs about your inheritance in *Love's Energy*?

> *It takes a whole person, a perfectly-imperfect person to catch this beat.*
>
> *As perfectly-imperfect people find out:*
>
> *We give and receive love as whole people and*
>
> *We discover the vastness of our ability to give and receive love.*
>
> *We step further into the vastness and might of Love's Energy.*
>
> *We no longer stop to enquire who is included.*
>
> *Our lookout is indiscriminate.*

What kind of love is giving by a God who does not discriminate? What a beautiful question to discover.

Love and Love's Energy

IS GOD REALLY LOVING?

"I may have convinced myself or been convinced by others that I deserve to be separated from God. Such lies will bring with them a shadow in which I experience a sense of separation, feelings that seem to validate the illusion that God is not connected and in relationship with me or that God has stopped loving me or has given up on me. Many of us on the planet live in this illusion now."
William Paul Young[1]

So many of us have been taught something about God that includes an idea of a stern figure looking down on us, seeing us flawed and inadequate. This image does not conjure a definition of a God who celebrates our beauty. And, being led to believe that God is looking down on us with acute scrutiny is usually introduced to us when we are very young.

From a young age, many people believe in a God who is full of shaming, scrutinizing, and condemning. It may actually be healthy to not want to be connected to such a god. Would we recommend any person continue this type of human relationship with a friend, or family member?

Somehow, we have gotten much more focused on the rules of godliness and all these rules have hindered our vision of *Love's Energy*. We think God is perfect and we think God loves rules, that God prefers to hand out stone tablets. *"And you get a stone tablet! And you get*

---

[1] Young, Wm. Paul (2017). Lies We Believe About God. Atria Books.

a stone tablet! And you get a stone tablet!" Of course, we get caught up in seeking the perfect plan to meet God's rules.

Personally, I like some of the rules in the Bible and I like some of the rules in the church. Some of them are good common sense. Some of them make life more straightforward. Like parenting and adulting, and life in general, some structure is helpful. A part of God loving us is that God does want us to live with moral insight.

Love's Energy advocates for God in this way:

> *God is sovereign. God is holy. God is our creator. God participates in our humanity. God is loving. God is loveable. God is indiscriminate. God includes all of as. God love's all of us. It is possible to love God.*

God is *"safe haven"* and *"secure base."*[1] That is to say *Love's Energy* is the template for our human offering of nurture. It is important to view God's love in terms of *"safe haven"* and *"secure base."* We are included in the same heart of love as everyone else. We choose what risks and adventures we take in our individual life. We make some good choices and some not-so-good. We are tattered and dappled, and then, hopefully, we are wiser and better, and whole. When we come back and check for certain that we are included, we always are. We are included when we are living our human life, and we are included when we are in contemplation and seeking of God. *Love's Energy* is the heartbeat continually connecting us to the heart of love.

---

[1] Clinton, Tim, Sibcy, Gary (2009). Attachments: Why You Love, Feel, and Act the Way You Do. Thomas Nelson.

Let's get this really clear. God's love is loving. God's love is including. God's love is God's heart. God's heartbeat is one we all know. God's heartbeat is what resounds through our human experience and reminds us of where we belong.

> Human love is a mirror of God's love.

When we hold a crystallized belief in *"fun police God,"* we don't get to experience this *Love's Energy* thing in full force. Hyperfocus on rules and religion is itself a default, it is another strategy to avoid our inner worries about who we are and all our individual flaws we know exist. It is another hindrance to our being in the fullness of our design. We have no eraser, and we have no need to erase any part of who we are. We are whole people wholly loved.

> God is not waiting for us to become worthy, so why are we?

Being religious about religion is not God. It does not make God more sovereign; we actually can't make God more sovereign, or more holy, or godlier. I think God has got this part all figured out. It is not our job to make God more like God.

> God oozes grace in connection with love.

We are loved by God. Our whole being is invited into this love embrace. Our flaws are invited into the heart of God's unyielding love. We are whole people who are wholly loved by God.

> God is really loving.

People who are offended by God's love do not know what love is. Love is not fluff. Love is scientifically proven to contribute to human evolution. God's love is hardwired into our biology; it benefits our neurology and our mental health.

It takes courage to learn what love is. Love is not a formula. Love is indiscriminate, inclusive, vulnerable, shameless, corrective, and soothing. And God really is loving us in these ways.

God does not discriminate. God is inclusive. God is safe. God is corrective. God is soothing. God is *Love's Energy*. God is sovereign. God is holy. God is God.

> *Love's Energy is the template for our love. Love's Energy is the heartbeat of God.*
>
> *Love's Energy is always supernatural.*

> There is something powerful evoked in me when I sit in the fullness of who I am knowing I am completely included and loved by God. I have learned as much as I am included today, I have always been. I don't need saving from a loving God who fully embraces me and has always embraced me. In the embrace of God's love, God meets me in my flaws. God is gentle and gracious to support me finding my footing in my human experience. God deeply cares about my old belief that I am heartless. God wants to support me to know my true identity, my *pure-of-heartness*.

I want other people to have this same experience.

> My old way, believing in a God waiting to scrutinize my every flaw, believing in a God who was waiting to reject me, sent me spiraling. It kept me afraid. It kept me longing for isolation. It kept me holding on to all the reasons why I

deserved a religious rejection, and it stopped me from holding on to the truth of me being included.

I belong to a loving God.

You belong to a loving God.

It really is a beautiful place to belong.

When we believe God is rejecting, we believe rejection is an option to live with in all of our relationships. All the while, looking for evidence of God rejecting us. This is a lonely set up. This is a lie.

God is always knowing us with a loving mind,

Always seeing us with loving eyes, and

Always hearing us with loving ears. That we may learn to greet ourselves in a similar manner, then greet others in this manner.

God is a great listener.

God has the most loving eyes.

God has the safest arms.

God has a familiar heartbeat.

God is always ready for us to remember how we are already included in Love's Energy. Get slow.

Get still. Do you hear it?

Can you catch the beat?

Is God really loving?

What if God is?

Love and Love's Energy

TYING IT IN A BOW

Love and Love's Energy

TREADING WATER

"Gratitude unlocks the fullness of life. It turns what we have into enough, and more. It turns denial into acceptance, chaos to order, confusion to clarity. It can turn a meal into a feast, a house into a home, a stranger into a friend. Gratitude makes sense of our past, brings peace for today and creates a vision for tomorrow." — Melody Beattie[1]

Most people love water. There is something about the look of water dancing in the sunlight, or the blanketing humidity on a pool deck, a warm bath at the end of a tiring day, or a quick shower to wake us in the morning. Beaches, swimming pools, fountains, ponds, fast boats, slow boats, river cruises, water sports, snorkeling, scuba diving, swimming, water draws us. For risk or tranquility, people love the water, or at least, we love the idea of water.

People love water and yet, when we do not learn to work with the water, we will fear it and fight it.

Water is so very much like love.

Like many of you I am a water person. I love swimming. I love working with the water below the surface and I love working with water to stay above its surface. As uncommon as this may sound, I even love treading water.

---

[1] Beattie, Melody (2022). Codependent No More: How To Stop Controlling Others and Start Caring for Yourself. Speigel & Grau

Playing.

Resting.

Swimming and

Letting the water swim through me.

Because of my love for performing the eggbeater with my legs, I think about the power of treading water and why so many people struggle with this style of swimming. For most people, treading water is excruciating work. People look exhausted and frustrated as they work their legs to keep their head above water. The irony is that treading water is not all too different from what we do when we try to live without *Love's Energy.*

I wondered why, when a boat capsizes, or people are struggling to keep their head above water, people instinctively tread water. It is easy to muster up an image of people with panic on their face, barely keeping their chins out of the waves as their legs kick under the dark blue surface of the ocean.

> We live our lives as if we are treading water.
>
> *Why don't we roll over and float on our backs?*

We work hard. We strategize systems of defaults, and we keep our chins out of the water. It is hard to trust life, so we keep treading water to stay above our surface. We realize we can't do this forever. We feel afraid we will not be able to keep this up as long as we need to. We feel our fear, and we are aware of how inadequate our technique to persevere. Our brain races through all the proof of why we are struggling more than the next person, all our flaws that hinder our effort. We are on our own in this struggle. Fighting our effort. Fighting our mind. Fighting our inner self.

> Why don't we roll over and float on our backs?

Floating is not a perfect solution. In ocean waves, it can prove quite difficult, at times impossible. Sometimes, we do need to tread water. After all, it is a lifesaving skill— our defaults are lifesaving skills at times too. But when we only tread water, we fight the water instead of slowing down to understand how to work with the water —in the same way we miss many opportunities when we don't slow down and notice how to work with love. The more frantically we persevere the more numerous the missed opportunities. There are many situations where it is quite natural to stop treading water and float in the water —in love. But will we allow ourselves to notice, will we allow ourselves to stop working so hard and to learn how to trust? *Will we roll over and float on our backs?*

> We rarely see anyone floating, especially adults.

Floating is a skill all its own. It is simple and it is not. It is a different method of working with the water. It is a skill to master, and it is frightening in its own way, until it is not. Floating on the water is learning to let go.

> We may never walk on water, but we can find rest on the water when we stop working so hard and roll over and *float*.

When we wade into a body of water, when we dive into a swimming pool, when we are tossed off the edge of a sinking ship, we are submerged in a great volume of water mass. Our body's mass is within the larger mass of the water. It may be natural to fight, but it is alright to be frightened. We will struggle at times.

> Water is a beautiful metaphor for *Love's Energy*. We are included in the larger mass of

> love, the same heart of love as everyone else, God's heart.

Like we do with water, we keep treading love instead of floating on our backs. We keep treading love, keeping our chins just above the surface. We default and we tread on the surface of love knowing we can't keep this up forever. When we labor this hard only to barely stay on its surface, then there is no option other than to feel flawed. Treading is a solo sport. It keeps us feeling alone in our efforts. Eventually we grow weak and tired. Exhausted on the surface of a love we barely know.

> Why don't we roll over and float on our backs?

What a beautiful image— floating on our backs, resting on the heart of love. Our ears submerged to hear the heartbeat of God. Our bodies relaxed. Our faces and minds turned upward. We don't need to worry about our flaws; they are fine. We don't need to struggle. We look up. We breathe. We think about taking a few moments under the surface. We catch the beat of love as we rest on love's mass, with our listening ears comfortably submerged. And we wonder about love.

What is also interesting is we might decide to grab the hand of someone who happens to be floating beside us. Floating is not a solo sport. It can be, but it is also fun to hold hands with a friend from time to time.

> We have had moments in this book where we have been floating on our backs. Some moments, you have been floating on your own, reveling in the vastness of this love pool. Other moments, you and I have linked up, we have held hands and took a float together.

May we be noticer of this vast pool of love that we are all included in.

We have always been in this great mass of love.

We are included in the same heart of love as everyone else.

Here we are loved, loveable, and loving.

Here we are

Heard by loving ears,

Seen by loving eyes, and

Known by the most loving mind.

Whether we tread water, or

float on our backs, or we are just learning to doggy paddle, we are participating.

Included.

Belonging.

We dive under the surface.

We tread water.

We float.

You are included in the same heart of love as everyone else.

You are loved, loveable, and loving.

You are heard by loving ears, you are seen by loving eyes, you are known by a loving mind.

And you do this for others, when you can as you can.

Will you fall into self-love?

Will you fall in love with others?

Will you look to see love-energy in the many ways it is revealed?

Will you float on your back and catch the heartbeat of love?

Will you float on your back and hold space to wonder about Love's Energy?

Will you let Love love you as it intends to?

Love and Love's Energy

A LETTER FROM WM. PAUL YOUNG

BEING LOVED

When Tara asked me to consider writing something about my experience of 'learning to be completely loved by God,' my first thought was, "What a great subject." My second thoughts right on the heels of my first were, "Have I learned to be completely loved by God?" and, "To whatever degree I have, how did I get here?"

Over the last week as I thought about this, I realized that experiencing God's love has been a slow, almost unnoticed burn, with plenty of hiccups along the way. For me, it hasn't been any sort of shattering event or revelation that settled the subject. And it continues. Also, it has required my choice and participation in the face of circumstances that I had not faced previously; the issue of finances in a difficult season, the death of two grandsons and the struggles of another, unanswered prayers, stupid choices, the challenges of health issues and of aging itself, and on and on and on. Each of these is part of the landscape in which I was given the choice to trust or to turn away from love.

To trust God is to experience being loved by God. To turn away to our own devices and control is to orient ourselves toward the shadowlands where our sense of God and Love is diminished, and we become lost and confused. Of course, God's love is always a constant, but in our turning and orientation away our awareness of that Love fades.

In the shadowlands, fear is a sniper that shoots into our heart whispers of abandonment, shame, distrust, and absence of Love. In the shadows it is difficult to perceive the right and the wrong, the good and the evil, the beautiful and the crass. But the redemption is that we are invited into the beautiful black where the true becomes clearer and more visible, for it is God who hovers over the dark within which the real and the right and the good await. We learn that Love was always present there and the invitation to re-turn is there with the expectancy of a waiting mother, to birth in us something deeper and newer and more mysterious; the maturing of our knowing of being Loved.

How have I learned to be completely loved by God? I haven't. But I am learning, and the road has been incremental, arduous, often painful and joy filled. And it is growing and maturing and deepening.

Laughter is the sister of tears, and both are conduits to re-turning, as is asking for forgiveness, becoming a truth-teller, and letting go of our addiction to control. God never turns, not even a shadow of turning. We turn and then we re-turn, again and again and again. And in each turning our knowing grows and since love is the skin of knowing, our love grows. And so too does our trust. Learning trust means we remain face to face as best we know how moment by moment and circumstance by circumstance.

Hugs,

Paul

Acknowledgements

I am everyone I have ever loved.

Thank you to those who have given me space to float in the giant mass of Love's Energy that we are all included in, and thank you to those who have floated with me and held my hand for a time.

As I participated in the creation of this beautiful book, you all were with me, and myriads of others. The participating I have experienced in the creation of this book has gifted me with a profound assurance of Love's Energy. I know where I am included. I know where I belong. I now know I have always been included and I have always belonged in this place of love. I hope you all will discover this truth as well.

Thank you, David Tensen, for publishing, editing and handholding, you have been the poet that eased my mind and nurtured my writer's heart; and to Felicia Murrell for editing this project; Thank you to my long-time friend and theology buddy Jared Robinson for your amazing cover art.

Thank you to all my friends, family and mentors:

John MacMurray thank you for building a table for us to meet at, and for all whom you have gathered at your open table; including Brad & Eden Jersak and William Paul Young, three people who continue to surprise me with their kindness and acceptance of me; Thank you to my friend David Hayward, a fellow contemplative, a pastor of love; and to the wise Ron Dart for introducing me to Thomas Merton, and for sharing your wit, wisdom and mind with me.

Gail Palmer, Jim Furrow and Robin Williams Blake, you all have been instrumental in keeping me in good community and teaching me how to tune in to attachment systems with clients, I would have given up long ago if not for you three; and to Ryan Rana, you are the real deal dude, you show up for people.

Thank you, Kent Hoffman, you helped me find my self, and attachment theory, and inspired me to know supernatural love is vaster and more brilliant than I could have guessed. I found my way back from the wilderness Kent. I hope you once more find the strawberry you need, and that, in sweetness, it will sing to you.

Thank you Dr's Paul and Lilian Wong, my mentors for life; to Dr. Kingsley Payne and Carolyn Lentz who supervised me to become a psychologist; to Team Sojourn come and gone, but always my dream team. Thank you to Lena you have encouraged me through the creation of this book; Lisa Rowbottom, you are a wise, steady companion, I am thankful to share "my Sojourn" with you.

And an immeasurable thank you to my business partners of almost 20 years Dan and Peggy Miller (aka mom and dad). Thanks for the love you have steadily given me. And thank you to my sister Lisa Wong for catching a last few edits, and for always offering "free hugs."

Thank you to all of my clients who have privileged me to hear you, to see you and to know you, just the way you are. Thank you for wrestling with me, and with yourselves. Keep on your love discovery, keep looking to see you are loved, loveable and loving; you are. And you are all in my heart.

Thank you Jason Boothby, you are a great love to have; this perfectly-imperfect love-energy of ours is sacred, and I am thankful for the love discovery of our marriage; we have earned and learned our love, a love that is worth keeping.

Elyana and Caedmon Edwin, I hope one day you will read mommy's book, but for now let's read all the other books, cuddle our sweet kitten Ponyo, and laugh at all the jokes and have millions of hugs. Mommy loves you Ely and Caed.

And a huge thank you to those of you who have read this book. And, thank you to those who have read this book and then recommend it to someone you love. I love this book, and it has been a blessing to share it with you.

Thank you for floating with me, and trusting me to lead you through this love discovery.

Want me to come visit your organization to discuss Love and Love's Energy?

Because I totally want to come see you! Shoot me an email: tara.boothby@sojo.ca

Love and Love's Energy

SUGGESTED READING AND BIBLIOGRAPHY

Ainsworth (Salter), Mary, Blehar, Mary C., Waters, Everett, Wall, Sally (1979). *Patterns of Attachment: A Psychological Study of the Strange Situation.* Routledge.

Alcoholics Anonymous World Services, Inc. (1989). *Twelve Steps and Twelve Traditions.* Alcoholics Anonymous World Services.

Amen, Daniel (2023). *Conquer Your Negative Thoughts: The secret to Emotional Freedom and Happiness.* Tyndale Refresh.

Beattie, Melody (2022). *Codependent No More: How To Stop Controlling Others and Start Caring for Yourself.* Speigel & Grau

Beattie, Melody (1990). *The Language of Letting Go: Daily Meditations on Codependency.* Hazelden Publishing.

Bernard Shaw, George (2001). *Man and Superman.* Penguin Classics (republished).

Boothby, Tara (2005). *The Young Love Project.* Thesis Research Trinity Wester University.

Bowlby, John. (1988). *A Secure Base: Parent-Child Attachment and Healthy Human Development.* Basic Books.

Bowlby, John. (1969). *Attachment and Loss: Volume 1*. Basic Books.

Bowlby, John, Fry, Margery, Slater Ainsworth, Mary D. (1953). *Child Care and the Growth of Love*. Penguin Books.

Bowlby, John. (1995). *Maternal Care and Mental Health*. Jason Aronson, Inc.

Bowlby, John. (2012). *The Making and Breaking of Affectional Bonds (Routledge Classics)*. Routledge.

Brown, Brené (2021). *Atlas of the Heart: Mapping Meaningful Connection and the Language of Human Experience*. Random House.

Brown, Brené (2015). *Rising Strong: The Reckoning, The Rumble. The Revolution*. Random House.

Brown, Brené (2010). *The Gifts of Imperfection: Let Go of Who You Think You're Supposed to Be and Embrace Who You Are*. Hazelden.

Brentherton I. (1992). *The Origins of Attachment Theory: John Bowlby and Mary Ainsworth*. Developmental Psychology, 63(6): 1456-1472.

Brimdyr, Kajsa: www.magicalhour.org.

Brown, Roger, Kulik, James (1977). *Flashbulb Memories*. Cognition 5 (1); 73-99.

Cannon, Walter B. (1963). *The Wisdom of the Body*. W.W. Norton & Company.

Clinton, Tim, Sibcy, Gary (2009). *Attachments: Why You Love, Feel, and Act the Way You Do*. Thomas Nelson.

Daines, Chantel L., Hansen, Dustin, Lelinneth B. Novilla, M., Crandall, AliceAnn (2021). *Effects of a Positive and Negative Childhood Experience on Adult Family Health.* BMC Health, Article number: 651.

DeBellis, Michael D; Woolley, Donald P., Hooper, Stephen R. (2013). *Neuropsychological Findings in Pediatric Maltreatment: Relationship of PTSD, Dissociative Symptoms, and Abuse/Neglect Indices to Neurocognitive Outcomes.* Child Maltreatment 18(3), 171-183.

Ekman, Paul, Friesen, Wallace V. (1975). *Unmasking The Face: A Guide to Recognizing Emotions From Facial Expressions.* Prentice-Hall.

Felitti, Anda, Nordenberg, Williamson, Spitz, Edwards, Marks. (1998). *Relationship of Childhood Abuse and Household Dysfunction to Many of the Leading Causes of Death in Adults: The Adverse Childhood Experience (ACE) Study.* American Journal of Preventive Medicine 14(4), 245-258.

Festinger, Leon (1954). *"A Theory of Social Comparison Processes." Human Relations, 7, 117-140.* Open House Journal of Social Sciences.

Frankl, Viktor E. (1959) *Man's Searching for Meaning.* Beacon Press.

Furrow, James L., Palmer, Gail, Johnson, Sue M., Faller, George, Palmer-Olsen, Lisa (2019). *Emotionally Focused Family Therapy: Restoring Connection and Promoting Resilience.* Routledge.

Gibran, Kahlil (1923). *The Prophet.* Alfred A. Knopf.

Goleman, Daniel (1995). *Emotional Intelligence: Why It Can Matter More Than IQ.* Bantam Books.

Gottman, John (2007). *And Baby Makes Three: The Six Step Plan for Preserving Marital Intimacy and Rekindling Romance After Baby Arrives.* Harmony.

Gottman, John (1997). *Raising An Emotionally Intelligent Child.* Simon & Schuster.

Gottman, John, DeClaire, Joan. (2001). *The Relationship Cure.* Harmony.

Gottman, John (2011). *The Science of Trust: Emotional Attunement for Couples.* Norton & Company.

Green, Michael (2013). *Quantum Physics and Ultimate Reality: Mystical Writings of Great Physicists.* Amazon Kindle Direct Publishing.

Hoffman, Kent (2015). *eightysevenminutes.com.*

Hoffman, Kent, Copper, Glen, Powell, Bert (2017). *Raising a Secure Child How Circle of Security Parenting Can Help You Nurture Your Child's Attachment, Emotional Resilience, and Freedom to Explore.* Guilford Press.

Holmes, Jeremy (1993). *John Bowlby and Attachment Theory (The Makers of Modern Psychotherapy.* Routledge.

Johnson, Sue (2019). *Attachment Theory in Practice: Emotionally Focused Therapy (EFT) with Individuals, Couples, and Families.* The Guilford Press.

Johnson, Sue (2008). *Hold Me Tight: Seven Conversations for a Lifetime of Love.* Little, Brown Spark.

Johnson, Sue (2013). *Love Sense: The Revolutionary New Science of Romantic Relationships.* Little, Brown Spark.

Johnson, Sue (2004). *The Practice of Emotionally Focused Couple Therapy: Creating Connections.* Routledge.

Kierkegaard, Soren (1849). *The Sickness unto Death.* Penguin Classics.

Le Leche League. *Breastfeeding After Caesarean Birth.* Llli.org/breastfeeding-info/breastfeeding-caesarean-birth/

Lewis, C.S. (1952). *Mere Christianity.* Geoffrey Bles.

Luther King, Jr., Martin (1986). *A Testament of Hope: The Essential Writings and Speeches.* HarperOne.

Main, Mary (2003). *Adult Attachment Scoring and Classification Systems (Version 7.2).* Department of Psychology, University of California, Berkeley.

Mandino, Og (1983). *The Greatest Salesman in the World.* Bantam; Reissue edition.

Marcel, Gabriel (1956). *The Philosophy of Existentialism.* Citadel Press.

Merton, Thomas (1950). *Seasons of Celebration: Meditations on the Cycle of Liturgical Feasts*. Farrar, Strays and Giroux, LLC.

Merton, Thomas (2002). *No Man Is an Island*. Harper Collins (republished).

Merton, Thomas (2004). *The Inner Experience: Notes on Contemplation*. HarperOne; Reprint edition.

Merton, Thomas (1948). *The Seven Storey Mountain*. Harcourt, Inc.

nakedpastor.com.

Neufeld, Gordon, Maté, Gabor (2006). *Hold On to Your Kids: Why Parents Need to Matter More Than Peers*. Ballentine Books.

Niebuhr, Reinhold (1941). *"The Serenity Prayer" Obituary. New York Herald Tribune*.

Noah, Trevor (2016). *Born A Crime: Stories From a South African Childhood*. Random House.

Paulsen, Sandra (2017). *When There Are No Words: Repairing Early Trauma and Neglect From the Attachment Period With EMDR Therapy*. CreateSpace Independent Publishing Platform.

Peterson, Eugene H. (1993). *The Message: The Bible in Contemporary Language*. NavPress.

Powell, Bert, Cooper, Glen, Hoffman, Kent (2016). *The Circle of Security: Enhancing Attachment In Early Parent-Child Relationships*. The Guilford Press.

Queen's University (2003, May 13). *Fetus Heart Races When Mom Reads Poetry: New Findings*

Reveal Fetuses Recognize Mother's Voice in-utero. www.sciencedaily.com/releases/2003/05/030513080440.htm.

Saint Augustine (2014). *The Four Books of St. Augustine on Christian Doctrine.* IndoEuropeanPublishing.com.

Seigel, Daniel J. (2020). *The Developing Mind: How Relationships and the Brain Interact to Shape Who We Are.* The Guilford Press.

Seigel, Daniel J., Hartzell, Mary (2013). *Parenting From The Inside Out: How a Deeper Self-Understanding Can Help You Raise Children Who Thrive.* TarcherPerigee; 10th Anniversary ed. Edition.

Siegel, Daniel, Payne Bryson, Tina (2011). *The Whole-Brain Child: 12 Revolutionary Strategies to Nurture Your Child's Developing Mind.* Delacorte Press.

Seuss, Dr. (1990). *Oh, The Places You'll Go!* Random House Books For Young Readers.

Smalley, Gary, Smalley, Greg, Smalley, Michael, Paul, Robert (2007). *The DNA of Relationships.* Tyndale House Publishers, Inc.

Thibaut, John W. (1986). *The Social Psychology of Groups.* Routledge.

Van der Kolk, Bessel (2014). *The Body Keeps The Score: Brain, Mind, and Body in the Healing of Trauma.* Viking Press.

Young, Wm. Paul (2017). *Lies We Believe About God.* Atria Books.

Young, Wm. Paul (2007). *The Shack: Where Tragedy Confronts Eternity.* Windblown Media, Faithwords, Hodder & Stoughton.

www.ingramcontent.com/pod-product-compliance
Lightning Source LLC
Chambersburg PA
CBHW031100080526
44587CB00011B/758